HEAVEN'S DOORS

Wider than you ever believed!

By George W. Sarris

GWS PUBLISHING Grace Will Succeed

GWS PUBLISHING Grace Will Succeed

Unless otherwise noted, Scripture quotations are taken from *The
Holy Bible, New International Version* (1984 Edition) copyright ©
1973, 1978, 1984 by Biblica, Inc. Used by permission.

ISBN 978-0-9800853-2-7 (Paperback Edition)
ISBN 978-0-9800853-3-4 (Ebook Edition)
ISBN 978-0-9800853-4-1 (Audio Book Edition)

Library of Congress Control Number: 2017901628

For speaking engagements, contact the author at
George@GeorgeWSarris.com

Editor, Jack Linn
Cover design by Fred Daunno

"George Sarris has performed a splendid service in tracing the Christian view of universal salvation, which has deep roots in the Bible and in the Church Fathers . . . The book is gracefully written, deeply thoughtful, and based on careful scholarship; it deserves the widest audience."

David Konstan, *Professor of Classics, New York University; Professor Emeritus of Classics and Comparative Literature, Brown University*

"I really, really, really enjoyed your writing style. You communicate in a way that draws others into the subject, and your views don't stomp on the considerations of others. It is engaging and friendly, and you use your real life circumstances and communications to illustrate your points."

Todd Hoyt, *CEO, EChristian/Christianaudio.com*

"EXCELLENT job. So well done . . . this could be the breakthrough book among Evangelicals and conservative Catholics especially . . . It is readable, clear, focused and free of red herrings and distracting baggage."

Brian McLaren, *Pastor, Author, Speaker*

"My view has changed. I find ultimate restoration as a reasonable position . . . I thank you deeply for opening my mind on eternal punishment/ultimate restoration."

Perry G. Phillips, *Author and Lecturer; MA Institute in Holy Land Studies, MDiv Biblical Theological Seminary, PhD Cornell University*

"Heaven's Doors is the kind of courageous look outside the theological box that some seldom questioned doctrines need. It comes from a seriously devoted follower of Christ with a high view of Scripture, so it needs a careful read."

Ed Morgan, *President and CEO, Bowery Mission, NY*

"Your terminological analysis (of *Hades, Gehenna, Tartarus, Sheol, Aionios, and Kolasis*) is quite sound. The historical survey is also correct . . . And you are absolutely right that the most ancient Creeds do not mention hell, let alone its eternity. They focus on the Good News!"

Ilaria Ramelli, *Professor of Theology and Bishop Kevin Britt endowed Chair in Dogmatics/Christology at the Graduate School of Theology at Sacred Heart Major Seminary of the Thomas Aquinas University; Onassis Senior Visiting Professor of Greek Thought and Church History at Harvard and Boston University; and Visiting Research Fellow at Oxford University*

"Evangelicals congratulate themselves on their willingness to submit to the final authority of scripture. Yet they also have cherished beliefs that they defend to the hilt . . . Quite rightly, George Sarris insists that even these beliefs should be subjected to the test of scripture. In this work he engages in detailed and challenging scrutiny of the biblical teachings on hell, eternal punishment and condemnation. Even those who do not agree with his conclusions need to pay attention to his arguments."

Nigel G. Wright, *Principal of Spurgeon's College, London; Council Member of Evangelical Alliance, UK*

"I know that if I had read this book earlier, I would have been going to church a lot more over the past 40 years!"

Fred Daunno, *Designer/Illustrator, lapsed Catholic and ordinary person*

For Suzan
My Darling Wife. My Dearest Friend.

Many women do noble things,
but you surpass them all!

Contents

Contents

Preface

What will happen to me and the people I love after we die?

At some point in nearly every person's life throughout history, people have wanted to know the answer to that question.

For the first 500 years after Christ, most Christians believed that God would ultimately redeem *all* of His creation. They believed Jesus Christ succeeded in His mission to seek and save the lost. The greatest story ever told was the greatest story that *could* ever be told!

Their answer to the question? You and all those you love will ultimately be in heaven.

Then, for the last 1,500 years, most of Christendom has been told that the majority of the billions of people who have lived on this earth will remain separated from the love and mercy of God for all eternity. The moms and dads, grandmas and grandpas, sons and daughters, relatives and friends who have not exhibited the "right kind" of faith here in this life will be shut up in a place called hell to suffer forever.

But is that really true?

Will more people suffer in hell eternally than live in heaven?

Is the greatest story ever told – the story of the creation, fall and redemption of mankind – really a tragedy for the vast majority of people who have ever lived . . . including many who you know and love?

Will most of the people God created in His image never walk through heaven's doors?

No!

That is a myth that was forced on the Christian Church by a power-hungry Roman emperor. It was supported by a highly respected but misinformed cleric. And it has endured for centuries because it became the status quo.

And it's time to expose that myth.

It wasn't always this way

During the first five centuries after Christ, many of the most prominent Christian leaders believed that hell was real, but it had a positive purpose. And it didn't last forever!

These early Christians include the man who wrote the first system of Christian theology. He's considered by many to be the most important theologian and Biblical scholar of the early Greek Church, a man named Origen.

Another man of great influence was Gregory of Nyssa, who was instrumental in defining the Christian doctrine of the Trinity that we still confess today. Gregory added the phrase *"I believe in the life of the world to come"* to the Nicene Creed, and was acknowledged in later centuries by the Church as "Father of the Fathers."

They and others believed that God doesn't defeat evil by shutting it up in a corner of His creation and leaving it there forever, like some kind of cosmic graveyard keeping sinners imprisoned for all eternity. Instead, they were convinced that God will destroy evil by transforming the hearts of evil-doers, ultimately making them into those who love goodness.

It was their understanding that at the end of time, God will actually get everyone He created into heaven.

Then, in the 6th century, the belief in hell as a place of never-ending, conscious torment was forced on the Church by the politically motivated Roman Emperor, Justinian I. He has often been called the "last Roman" because of his zeal to revive the empire's greatness and his declaration that the Emperor's will is law.

He was supported by the writings of one of the most revered and loved of all early theologians, the man known as St. Augustine. Unlike Origen, Gregory and others before him who read the New Testament in their native language, Augustine was unable to read Greek. He therefore based his belief in endless punishment on an incorrect Latin translation of the text instead of the original language.

In the centuries that followed, the belief that hell was punishment that would never end provided justification for those in the religious establishment to persecute and even torture any and all who disagreed with their views. Some had sincere but misguided motives. Others sought power, position and wealth.

For the past 1,500 years, most of Christendom has been told that history ultimately ends tragically. Many are saved. But most are lost forever.

Why has the myth persisted?

One of the most common responses I get when I tell this to people is,

"Why have I never heard this before? I'd certainly like to believe that what you're saying is true. But I can't believe that you would be the only person in the last 1,500 years to have discovered this!"

First of all, I'm not the only person in the last 1,500 years to "discover" this. The Eastern Church never lost sight of this truth. And in the Western Church there have been many individuals and groups throughout Church history who have been convinced that God will ultimately restore all.

William Law, a clergyman who influenced John Wesley and the evangelical revival in 18th century England, believed it. So did Benjamin Rush, a signer of the Declaration of Independence and co-founder of the Philadelphia Bible Society. Their voices, and those of many others over time, spoke the message. But they were drowned out by louder voices. The truth was never lost. It was only hidden.

Second, the reason why most people have never heard this is really quite simple.

Intimidation led to fear, which resulted in ignorance in future generations.

When influential Church authorities declared that hell was never-ending misery for those who didn't follow their teaching, many began to believe what they were told.

Once that declaration was accompanied by action – persecution and torture in the days of the Inquisition, and the threat of excommunication or ostracism in later times – people became very wary of challenging what the authorities said. As fewer and fewer questioned the tradition, people began to assume it was true. They either ignored or were unaware of views that disagreed with what they had been told.

That intimidation and fear continue to exist in our world today.

When I began writing this book, I knew my beliefs would be controversial, even though they're based on extensive historical and Biblical research that's been endorsed by world-renowned scholars.

What I didn't know was that I would lose dear friends. I would lose business colleagues I had worked with for years. I would lose my job with a Christian ministry I had worked with for almost 10 years. And my family and I would lose our church where we had been active members for 20 years. All because people found out I was writing a book about God's love for all mankind.

A pastor friend of mine made the mistake of letting officials in his denomination know of his belief that God will ultimately reconcile all of creation to Himself. He was tried, found guilty and defrocked.

Another friend who holds a leadership position in his denomination recently told me he thought he'd look into this issue when he retires in a few years – after he no longer has to worry about having to step down from his position.

I've had numerous email interactions with a person who believes strongly that God will ultimately restore all. To this day, he has never told me his name or where he lives because he's afraid people in his church might learn of it, and he and his family would have to leave.[1]

People are very hesitant to question the traditional belief that's been handed down to them, even though they may feel uncomfortable with that belief. It's not that they've rejected a Biblical argument for ultimate restoration. They've never heard it!

What do you believe?

The God who created the world is all-powerful. He is all-wise. He is all-loving. And this Creator has specifically said He wants all people to be saved and come to the knowledge of the truth.

So why should it be hard to believe that God will actually accomplish what He said He desires to do? Jesus Christ did *not* fail in His mission to seek and save what was lost. He's the Savior of the world, not just the Savior of a small part of the world. Have you wondered where you and those you love will go when you die?

Read the book, and ask yourself what you think.

Heaven's doors really may be wider than you ever believed!

Chapter 1

How much are you worth?

The look in his eyes and the tone in his voice let my brother and me know that what our father was about to tell us was important. Really important. It was something we needed to know. It was something we wanted to hear.

I was seven. My brother was five. We were sitting on the front seat of our old blue Plymouth on the road from the small town where we lived in upstate New York to an even smaller town five miles away. There were no seat belts back then, but we knew that if the car stopped suddenly, Dad would automatically stretch out his arm – like he always did – to protect us from being thrown forward.

"Do you know how much I love you?" Dad asked.

"How much?" We answered.

"All the way up to the sky and back again . . . 934,687,432 times . . . and more!"

"Wow!"

Over the years, Dad would ask us that question over and over again. The specific number would change, but it would always include *and more.* That was the key. We had no idea how far away the sky was, or how big those numbers were. But the idea that our father's love for us was more than the greatest distance and the biggest number we had ever heard, made it clear that we were truly loved. Our father's love for us was unlimited!

I will always be grateful to God for the father He gave me. He wasn't perfect. He made many of the same mistakes that other fathers make. But he was a good man. I always knew he loved me. I always knew he wanted the best for me. And no matter how much I messed up, I always knew he would never give up on me or abandon me.

My father taught me how to be a dad. He taught me how to love my wife and children. He taught me, by his example, about God's unlimited, unconditional, never-ending love for all mankind.

This book is about our heavenly Father's love for His children. Not just for a few. It's about His love for *all* His children. The God of the Bible will ultimately embrace the souls of all He created and open heaven's doors to everyone!

What's the big deal?

This is a book about hope. It's a book about truth. It's a book about unlimited power and unfailing love working together to accomplish the greatest plan ever conceived. This is a book about God's plan to ultimately get each and every person into heaven!

But why is that such a big deal?

A lot of people live in this world. You live in it. I live in it. Your family, your friends, your neighbors, your coworkers, even those you don't like live in it. Some have the same skin and hair color that you have. Many do not. Some live in the same part of the world you live in. Many do not. Some eat the same foods you eat, wear the same kinds of clothes you wear, and believe the same things you believe. Many do not.

But every one of them was created by God and placed on this earth.

Right now the world population numbers about 7 billion. That's a lot of people! Of that number, about a third – or roughly 2.3 billion people – call themselves *Christians* in one way or another. That includes liberal and conservative Protestants, strict and not-so-strict Roman Catholics, members of a variety of Eastern Orthodox churches, and just about everyone you can think of who claims to follow Christ in some fashion.

But even if all those who say they are Christians really are true believers, that would mean that well over *4 billion people* are currently outside the faith – the vast majority of whom will never profess Christ in their lifetime. What's more astonishing is that more than *2 billion people* live in places where the name of Jesus Christ is completely unknown!

Are all those people destined to suffer in hell forever when they die?

An uncomfortable belief

Although most Christians today believe hell is unending misery for most people, it's something we don't like to talk about openly or even think about. Some of us are like a friend who told my wife that she'd always wondered about hell but was afraid to look into it too carefully because she thought she'd get discouraged.

Others think about it when they look at non-believers who are prospering in this world. Some are actually glad they believe in hell when someone's hurt them deeply or mocked them for their faith. In that case, they gain a degree of satisfaction in thinking that the godless will eventually "get what they deserve!"

But have you ever had to comfort someone who lost a dear family member or friend who died without ever making a profession of faith? Has someone very close to you died in that same way? What did you say? When that happens, about the only comforting thing you can say to your friend or yourself is that you don't really know what occurred in the final seconds of the loved one's life. Who knows? Maybe they made peace with God at that time.

I recently talked with a man who told me he stopped believing in God and going to church when he heard that most of his friends and a lot of people in other parts of the world who had never heard of Jesus were going to hell. He decided then that he just couldn't believe in a God who was that uncaring! He now professes to be a Buddhist.

Christians often talk of and sing praises about the wonderful, never-ending love of God in church services, Bible studies, and personal interaction with other believers.

But if we honestly believe what we've been told to believe, we'd have to admit that those songs and words are not entirely accurate. God doesn't really love with an everlasting love. His love is conditional. His love is limited. For those who haven't professed faith in Him here in this life, God's love and mercy end at the moment of death.

A controversial book

This is not a safe book.

People take their religious beliefs very seriously, as they should. And beliefs that have been held by people for 100s of years through generation after generation of influence by family members, friends and religious leaders are very hard to change, regardless of how those beliefs have been impacted by misinterpretation or manipulation – innocent or not.

Some people will love this book and want to tell all their friends about it. Some will hate it and try to keep others from reading it. Many will welcome an honest book that challenges the traditional teaching from a clear, Biblical and historical perspective. Others, including some who will never actually read it, will call it heresy.

So how should you approach what I have to say? Let me suggest two underlying thoughts that I've found very helpful over the years in dealing with controversial issues.

The first is to remember that every book you will ever read about God and the Bible, including this one, has been written by a human being. And human beings are just that. They're human. Not everything they think or say is right. Many of the great theologians of the past and present were or are dedicated, brilliant individuals. But to err is human. Some of their ideas may be incorrect.

The second thing I try to keep in mind is that when two wise, godly individuals differ on an important issue, tread lightly. One of the two may be right and the other wrong. But it may also be true that both are right and both are wrong . . . and that a third alternative that neither has really considered may ultimately reconcile the two.

The focus of this book is what I would call the *third alternative*. It's a view, clearly based on history and the Bible, that most people today have never really considered.

Reading this book has the potential to change the way you look at people, especially those who ridicule or ignore you, or those whose lifestyles and values are offensive to you.

People are not the enemy. They are not individuals who need to be persuaded that you are right and they are wrong. They're not people whose lives may be important for a while, or even for a lifetime, but who are ultimately meant to be thrown away. People are created beings of inestimable worth who need to be rescued by God from pursuing wasted, meaningless lives.

Reading this book also has the potential to change the way you look at God, especially if you've wondered how an all-powerful, all-wise Being whose love is everlasting, could cause or allow anyone to experience conscious, endless suffering with no hope for restoration.

God is *not* a tender-hearted but ultimately weak Being who created a universe that was *very good* in the beginning but ends up *almost very good* – or even worse, *not very good* in the end. God is *not* an all-powerful Despot who chooses some to live forever in luxury beyond description, while others are chosen to experience for all eternity a degree of degradation that is too horrendous for our finite minds to even conceive.

On the contrary . . . God is far greater, far more powerful, and far more wonderful than you or I have ever thought or imagined. He defeated sin and death completely and will one day see *all* those He created walk through heaven's doors.

Where are we going?

Is hell a place of conscious suffering that never ends, where billions of people will cry out for endless ages?

> "Father of Mercies! Why from silent earth
> Didst thou awake and curse me into birth!
> Tear me from quiet, ravish me from night,
> And make a thankless present of Thy light?
> Push into being a reverse of Thee,
> And animate a clod with misery?"[2]

No! God does not give up on any of those He created. He is wise enough, loving enough and powerful enough to accomplish the full redemption of all His creatures!

Before you read further, let me answer some quick questions that you may be asking.

Does the book teach that hell does not exist? No! Hell does exist, but for a good purpose. And it doesn't last forever.

Does the book teach cheap grace? No again. No one gets a free ticket to heaven! Because punishment in hell is not endless, does not mean that God's judgments are not real. After-death punishment is both severe and intense for those who continue to resist God's grace.

Does the book teach that hell is really Purgatory, where works of penance are a substitute for the work of Christ? No. It's only because of the cross of Jesus Christ that anyone can be saved. Physical death doesn't mark the end of when God works in people's hearts. He continues to work even after we die.

Does the book teach that repentance and faith are unnecessary? No. All will eventually be saved because all will eventually repent and believe.

Does the book teach that everyone God has created will eventually be in heaven? Yes! Evil will not remain a part of God's creation forever. At the end of time, all those who God created will experience the peace and joy of being in His presence.

If you're like most people I've talked to, much of the material in this book will be completely new to you. Some of it may seem a little technical at first, but it's important! It's information you need to know to come to an informed conclusion. I hope and pray all of it will be interesting and encouraging.

I've worked hard trying to take a big topic and communicate it in simple and easy to read language. For those of you who want more details, you'll find them in

Endnotes at the back of this book. My only request is that you actually read the book before making any judgments.

You may be surprised to see how wide heaven's doors really are!

The real issue

How much are you worth?

I don't mean that in any financial sense such as, "What is your *net* worth?" I mean how much are you worth *as a person?* How much are you worth to those who love you? How much are you worth to God?

I posed that question over and over again to each of my children, starting when they were just old enough to talk. I wanted to instill in them a vital truth about their real value to me as their father – and to God as their heavenly Father. Just as my father taught me, I wanted to teach each of my children that they were of unlimited value.

"How much are you worth?" I would ask. The answer from my children was always the same. *"I'm priceless!"*

That's not only how valuable my children are. That's how valuable *you* are. That's how valuable *every person who has ever lived* is to God.

You and they are priceless!

Chapter 2

What are we talking about anyway?

The family was sitting around their dinner table when the oldest son told everyone about a conversation he had earlier that day with his friend, Johnny. Johnny didn't go to church and said he didn't believe in God.

"I told him that if he didn't believe in God, he would go to hell!" the son had said.

That comment didn't sit well with his younger sister, and she quickly retorted,

"Daddy, that's a bad word, and you shouldn't let him say it!"

Children are often very careful to make sure their parents or their siblings don't do something they're not supposed to do.

"We definitely shouldn't use that word carelessly," the father answered. *"And it's probably not a good idea to tell your friend that he's going to hell,"* he said to his son. *"But do you know why?"*

The children looked at each other cautiously, then back to their father. The oldest son, especially, had wanted to ask his dad about hell for a while but was afraid he'd get into trouble if he said something.

"Hell is a very serious subject with very serious implications," the father explained. *"If what people say about it is true, it's worse than the worst thing you can think of."*

His daughter whispered quietly, *"Jenny told me that hell is the place where bad people suffer forever and ever after they die. Is that true?"*

"That's a good question," her father answered. *"In fact, it's a question everyone should ask before they tell someone else they're going to hell."*

What do Christians believe?

Children often say profound things. And a pretty good definition for hell is the one given by Jenny. Hell is a place or condition of *conscious misery* that *never ends*.[3]

Interestingly, that's not how hell has always been understood. It may come as a surprise, but there have actually been three very different views held by sincere Christians through the ages about the nature and duration of hell.

The first view is Jenny's – the traditional view. Once people die, the final judgment takes place, and there is no hope for those who didn't repent and believe during their lifetime on earth. Their punishment is never-ending.

A second view teaches that sometime after death, the bodies, souls and spirits of those in hell will be completely destroyed. They will become non-existent. It's called conditional immortality or annihilation.

The third view – and the one you'll read about in this book – is that hell is temporary and has a purpose other than inflicting pain. God will use it to bring people to a point where they acknowledge their need for Him and His saving grace in Jesus Christ. At some time in the future, perhaps the very distant future, those in hell will ultimately be restored to fellowship with God. This view has been called by various names – universalism, universal reconciliation, universal restoration, or the term that I prefer, ultimate restoration.

There are people today, as in the past, who hold to each of these positions. But Jenny's view is clearly dominant.[4] By contrast, the belief in some kind of ultimate restoration is widely considered to be a pie-in-the-sky, weakly supported belief held primarily by people who may have good hearts, but who clearly don't base their beliefs on the Bible.[5]

Who goes to hell?

If you've ever attended a Bible study, Sunday school class or some other activity where people get together to discuss serious issues of faith, you may have heard a debate between those who believe that God *predestines* certain people to be saved, and others who believe that mankind has *free will*. I've participated in many of these discussions over the years, and sometimes the arguments can get quite heated. That's because it's a question about who actually decides who goes to heaven and who goes to hell.

Is it God . . . or is it me?

For those who see God as all-powerful, it's absolutely clear that nothing ultimately happens in this universe that He has not predetermined. So when it comes to salvation, God must be the One who decides. Those who have not been chosen by God for heaven will suffer forever in hell after they die.[6]

However, for those who see God as loving, it's just as clear that He does not show favoritism or partiality.

Therefore, He offers the gift of salvation to all, but some decide they don't want it. If I reject His offer in this life, I will go to hell.

Just about everyone I've talked to or read on the subject agrees that never-ending, conscious suffering for anyone is the most dreadful event conceivable. However, they feel forced to their conclusion because of what they see as the clear teaching of the Bible, and especially because of the teachings of Jesus Christ on the matter. Most also maintain that it was the common opinion of the majority of those in the ancient church.

What do you think?

In my experience, most Christians today are very hesitant about telling others what they believe about hell. That was not the case, however, with many of our predecessors. They did not mince words!

For example, consider the words of one of the best known preachers and theologians of Protestant church history, Jonathan Edwards. His sermons began the First Great Awakening in America in the 1730s and 40s, and he is widely considered to be one of the greatest thinkers America has produced.

"Do but consider what it is to suffer extreme torment forever, and ever to suffer it day and night, from one day to another, from one year to another, from one age to another, from one thousand ages to another, and so, adding age to age, and thousands to thousands, in pain, in wailing and lamenting, groaning and shrieking, and gnashing your teeth; with your souls full of dreadful grief and amazement, with your bodies and every member full of racking torture, without any possibility of getting ease; without any possibility of moving God to pity by your cries; without any possibility of hiding yourselves from him; without any possibility of diverting your thoughts from your pain; without any possibility of obtaining any manner of mitigation, or help, or change for the better any way....

"After you shall have worn out a thousand more such ages, yet you shall have no hope, but shall know that you are not one whit nearer to the end of your torments; but that still there are the same groans, the same shrieks, the same doleful cries, incessantly to be made by you . . . which will not have been at all shortened by what shall have been past."[7]

Is that what you believe?

A little over a century later, another great preacher and theologian, Charles Spurgeon, challenged his audience with these words.

"There is a place, as much beneath imagination as heaven is above it; a place of murky darkness, where only lurid flames make darkness visible; a place where beds of flame are the fearful couches upon which spirits groan . . . there is a place where the only music is the mournful symphony of damned spirits; where howling, groaning, moaning, wailing and gnashing of teeth, make up the horrid concert. There is a place where demons fly, swift as air, with whips of knotted burning wire, torturing poor souls; where tongues, on fire with agony, burn the roofs of mouths that shriek for drops of water – that water all denied . . .

"Ah! sinners, if you knew what hell meant, then might ye tell what it is to lose your own souls."[8]

Spurgeon was the foremost preacher of his day and is

still the most widely read preacher in history. In 1861, before the modern megachurches of today that seat thousands, Spurgeon's congregation built The Metropolitan Tabernacle which seated 4,700 people. In that same year, he preached at London's Crystal Palace to a congregation of 23,654 people without the aid of a microphone or any other means of amplification.

Do Spurgeon's words reflect the belief that exists in your heart?

Most people today, including many devout Christians, feel embarrassed when they read or hear such hellfire-and-brimstone preaching. We don't like to talk about hell, and when pressed by someone who questions it, we usually explain that it's not a place of literal fire and torment. We'd prefer to describe the suffering and pain more abstractly as a state of loss or separation from God. Many feel more comfortable saying that it may not be inflicted pain, but felt pain.

But any way you say it, it still requires the belief that billions of people will experience unending misery. And as the little girl's father pointed out, it's definitely a serious subject, with very serious implications, that if true is worse than the worst thing you can think of.

The end of the matter

Because endless punishment has been preached so fervently by so many people for so long a time, most Christians today consider the idea of ultimate restoration to be a great error held only by those who are, at best, motivated by tender but misguided feelings. At worst, they believe it to be false teaching that gives false hope to ignorant and unwary people, and therefore must be guarded against at all cost.

But are they correct?

Is the hope that God will ultimately restore all, a great evil that must be stamped out? Am I, along with others who hold to that position, a wicked person who is preaching a different gospel? Or are many, like the Pharisees of old, actually nullifying the Word of God by holding to the traditions of men?

Edward Beecher, noted 19th century theologian, pastor, and brother of Harriet Beecher Stowe, challenged his contemporaries over a century ago. He said punishing people endlessly *"would be an extreme of injustice and cruelty that would entirely transform the character of God."*[9]

John Wenham, a well-respected 20th century evangelical scholar and preacher explained his concerns in these words.

> "Unending torment speaks to me of sadism, not justice. It is a doctrine which I do not know how to preach without negating the loveliness and glory of God. From the days of Tertullian it has been the emphasis of fanatics. It is a doctrine that makes the Inquisition look reasonable. It all seems a flight from reality and common sense."[10]

So, is belief in endless punishment the clear teaching of Scripture and a doctrine that must be strenuously argued for? Or is there support within the Bible and the teaching of Christians throughout history for a belief in ultimate restoration?

Let's look and see.

One last thought

"Dad, Johnny's my best friend, and I like him a lot. We argue sometimes, and sometimes even get into fights. But I don't think I'd like to see him suffer forever. Do you think God can save Johnny, too?"

"Yes, I do, sweetheart."

"Dad? I never told you this. But Grampa told me once he didn't believe in God, either."

Chapter 3

Where did endless punishment come from?

"This morning, just before noon, I received a phone call from the chaplain of the Bay Front Medical Center in St. Petersburg, FL.

"He informed me that my mother had been involved in a serious car accident in Sarasota, and had been flown by helicopter to the trauma center in St. Petersburg. She was in critical condition. He didn't know much else – about my father, whether he was involved, how he was, etc.

"I phoned the State Police in Sarasota, and learned that my father, along with my aunt Helen, had been killed in the accident, and Uncle John was also injured. I called my brother, and we both arranged to fly down tonight. I met Brian in Philadelphia, and we flew on the same flight into Tampa.

"My mom has a ruptured spleen, several broken ribs, deflated lung, bones out of joint in her hand, bruised heart and much swelling. The doctor had expected her to die, but she made it through! She is conscious, nodding in answer to questions.

"Lord God, please give her physical strength, encourage her spirit, and make Your presence more real to her now than at any time before in her life.

"Thank You for my father – I loved him so very much."

Those are the words I wrote in my journal the day my father died.

He and my mom were on their way to visit one of my mother's sisters when the accident occurred. The attending physician at the trauma center gave my mom a 2 to 3% chance of living when she arrived. God was gracious and she miraculously pulled through. When my brother and I were assured that she had stabilized enough for us to leave, we flew back to our homes and made arrangements for our father's funeral.

It's been said that there are only two things in this life that we can be sure of. In reality, there's only one.

My father died in that car accident. My mother died 18 years later. Someday I will die. Someday you will die. Someday everyone you know and everyone you don't know will die. It makes no difference if we are rich or poor, wise or foolish, educated or uneducated, successful or unsuccessful. We are mortal, and we are going to die.

For that reason, death has always occupied the minds of the living. Particularly, what happens *after* we die? That's a question that everyone thinks about at one time or another. That's the question everyone wants to know the answer to.

Contrary to popular opinion, however, the idea that some people will be tortured and suffer in hell forever after they die did *not* come from the Bible! It is not originally a Judeo-Christian concept at all, even though most people today think of it that way.

Punishments in the Old Testament

People often say that the God of the Old Testament is a God of wrath, while the God of the New Testament is a God of love. That's not true. God is One. He does not change. He is the same yesterday, today and forever.

Throughout the pages of the Old Testament, there is nothing that even remotely resembles the descriptions I quoted in the last chapter from the hellfire-and-brimstone sermons of Jonathan Edwards and Charles Spurgeon.

It does not talk of a

> "place of racking torture without any possibility of getting ease or moving God to pity by your cries."

There is no mention of a place where

> "demons fly swift as air with whips of knotted burning wire, torturing poor souls."

There is nothing that even comes close to images of a

> "horrid concert made up of the mournful symphony of damned spirits howling, groaning, moaning, and wailing throughout all eternity."

The Old Testament *does* talk of punishment for sins. God deals decisively with those who pervert justice, and whose behavior will ultimately bring pain and sadness to themselves and others. But the only form of divine punishment prominently presented from the creation of Adam to Israel's return to the Promised Land, was punishment meted out on this earth. It didn't refer to the spirit world or a future state.

25

For example, the first instance of punishment mentioned in the Bible, pronounced on Adam and Eve in the Garden of Eden, was natural death. God told Adam not to eat fruit from the forbidden tree. If he did, he would die. Adam disobeyed. He ate fruit from the forbidden tree. And he died.

There were certainly additional consequences that resulted from their disobedience. A sense of shame led Adam and Eve to hide from God and cover themselves with fig leaves. The ground produced thorns and thistles, making Adam's work harder when he tried to farm the land. And Eve experienced pain in childbirth. But the main thrust of the punishment was clear – *"for dust you are and to dust you will return."*[11]

The punishment was physical death. It occurred in this life. The consequences lasted until they returned to the ground.

The same is true throughout Scripture. The wicked in Noah's day died when the flood came upon the earth. The cities of Sodom and Gomorrah were physically destroyed and their inhabitants killed in the judgment that befell them. The plagues on Egypt laid waste to the land and brought physical death to all their firstborn sons. Jesus referred to the flood and the destruction of Sodom as illustrations and warnings of the coming judgments on Jerusalem.[12]

But they were events that occurred in this life.

So were the blessings and curses of the Law. Leviticus 26 and Deuteronomy 28 promised health, long life, fruitful seasons, military ascendancy, honor and power for Israel if she walked in the ways of the Lord. It threatened disease, famine, defeat in war, shame and weakness if she chose to disobey the Lord. The periods of the judges and kings illustrate graphically how these punishments were meted out. They happened in the here and now of life on earth.

In all their warnings against wickedness and idolatry, the great prophets Isaiah, Jeremiah and Ezekiel didn't refer to future punishments in the spirit world or to some kind of redemption from them. They referred to the terrors of the siege, of famine, of the capture of the city, of captivity in a strange land, or to their being brought back from such captivity.

Again, these were all things that occurred on this earth, in this life.[13]

Many Bible teachers suggest that natural disease and death should be seen as symbolic of spiritual disease and death. But there's nothing at all in the Biblical texts to indicate that this is how they were intended to be understood. The earthly punishments are set forth and proclaimed without any reference to the spiritual world and a future state. God said He would execute judgment on earth, and He did what He said He would do.[14]

So, what does the Old Testament teach about hell?

In the words of one contemporary scholar, *"Very little."*[15] As far as the future judgment of the wicked is concerned, all that is said explicitly in the Old Testament is that they will depart to *Sheol* – the place of the dead – not knowing what their ultimate fate will be.[16]

What did the pagans think?

The fact that everyone eventually dies is undeniable. Every person, in every culture, at every time in history has understood that. Coupled with that fact is another unquestionable reality.

Life just isn't fair!

Injustices and inequities are part of life in this world. And inherent in all of us is a sense that somehow, something has to be done in the *next* world that will rectify the unfairness we see all around us in *this* world.

27

Throughout history, people in every culture have wrestled with what that might look like and tried to come up with an answer. Most have concluded that there is some kind of balance scale on the other side on which humans are weighed. Those who are worthy will go to a place of great blessing. Those who are found wanting will be cast into a place of anguish and misery.

That was clearly the case with the ancient Egyptians, Babylonians, Greeks and Romans. Each had a fairly well-developed idea of what would happen to the wicked when they died. And each was very close to the traditional view of hell.

For example, in an ancient Egyptian tomb from the 20th Dynasty,[17] there is a text that has come to be known as the *Book of Caverns.* It was written on a wall inside a tomb so the deceased person could read it easily after he died. It describes the journey of the sun god through the six caverns of the underworld.

In the lowest part of the sixth section, we see pictures of goddesses wielding knives, torturing figures whose heads are set at their feet and whose hearts have been torn from their bodies. The accompanying text explains that the souls and shadows of these beings have also been punished.

The second scene shows four bound female enemies who are guarded by two jackal-headed goddesses. Re, the sun god, has condemned them to the *"Place of Annihilation, from which there is no escape."*[18]

An account from ancient Babylon and Assyria tells of the descent of the goddess Ishtar into the netherworld. Ishtar is the goddess of life and fertility. She descends into the land of no return to the place where the goddess of death and sterility dwells.

"To the house which those who enter cannot leave,

On the road where traveling is one-way only,
To the house where those who enter are
deprived of light,
Where dust is their food, clay their bread.
They see no light, they dwell in darkness ...
Over the door and the bolt, dust has settled."[19]

The Greek writer Plato told his readers about a place in
the depths of the earth filled with great rivers of fire. It's a
dreadful place where those who have committed gross sins
are cast. It's also a place from which these wicked sinners
will never depart.

"There are everlasting rivers of huge size under
the earth, flowing with hot and cold water; and
there is much fire, and great rivers of fire . . .
those who appear to be incurable, on account
of the greatness of their wrongdoings, because
they have committed many great deeds of
sacrilege, or wicked and abominable murders,
or any other such crimes, are cast by their
fitting destiny into Tartaros, whence they never
emerge."[20]

The Roman author Virgil also writes of a place of deep
distress and sadness.

"The gates of hell are open night and day;
Smooth the descent, and easy is the way...
Just in the gate and in the jaws of hell,
Revengeful Cares and sullen Sorrows dwell,
And pale Diseases, and repining Age,
Want, Fear, and Famine's unresisted rage;
Here Toils, and Death, and Death's half-brother,
    Sleep,
Forms terrible to view, their sentry keep."[21]

Unlike what we find in the Old Testament, these texts
sound a lot like the descriptions in the hellfire-and-

brimstone sermons we looked at earlier. They talk of *supernatural beings torturing the souls of men and women.* They tell of a place where *darkness dwells and from whence there is no escape.* They speak of *rivers of fire* and a place where the inhabitants are filled with *revengeful cares and sullen sorrows.*

But they were written thousands of years before those preachers ever lived. And they were written by people who had little or no contact with the Bible.

The time between the Testaments

Although it was definitely not taught in the Old Testament, a developed view of the afterlife did arise among the Jews during the four centuries before the coming of Christ. It was a time of great upheaval when the nation of Israel was ruled by the Persian, Greek and Roman empires. The thinking during this time increasingly bore the influence of many years of contact with those cultures.

One of the clearest statements in this Jewish literature about what will happen after death is found in chapter 7 of a book called 2 Maccabees. It's the account of the martyrdom of a mother and her six sons. The second son expresses a clear hope of resurrection from the dead as he says to his torturer,

> "You accursed fiend, you are depriving us of this present life, but the King of the world will raise us up to live again forever. It is for his laws that we are dying."

Later in the same chapter, the fourth brother adds his confident belief that the wicked will not enjoy those same blessings of the resurrection.

> "It is my choice to die at the hands of men with the God-given hope of being restored to life by him; but for you, there will be no resurrection to

life."

The Wisdom of Solomon is another well-known Jewish work of that time. It again teaches that the hope of the righteous is *"full of immortality."*[22] However, it goes a step beyond what the brothers asserted in 2 Maccabees. Not only will there be no resurrection to life for the wicked, the writer tells us that the wicked will actually be punished, although what that punishment is, isn't spelled out in detail. All that's said is that it will be just.

> "The wicked shall receive a punishment to match their thoughts, since they neglected justice and forsook the Lord."[23]

The belief expressed in the Book of Enoch, another non-Biblical writing from this period, comes the closest to speaking of hell in a way similar to what we have come to associate with that term. It warns sinners that

> "Into darkness and chains and a burning flame where there is grievous judgment shall your spirits enter; and the great judgment shall be for all the generations of the world. Woe to you, for ye shall have no peace."[24]

Justice will come to those who have done wicked things. The spirits of these wicked individuals will be sent into darkness and a burning flame.

But please note. The ideas of the afterlife expressed here are actually much closer to those expressed by pagan writers in the ancient world than they are to the Old Testament or even most of the non-Biblical Jewish literature.

The Time of Christ

Throughout history, there have been liberals, conservatives and independents, not only in politics but in religion as well.

Although contemporary labels don't fit exactly, in Jesus' time a group called the Sadducees were what many today would consider religious liberals. They were associated with the Temple in Jerusalem and generally represented the upper social and economic echelon of Judean society.

A group called the Pharisees were what many would consider religious conservatives. They focused on adhering to oral tradition in addition to the written law in an attempt to make sure people didn't do things they weren't supposed to.[25]

The Sadducees didn't believe in a resurrection to heaven or future punishment in hell. The Pharisees believed in both.

The extent of the disagreement between these two groups can be seen in the quarrel that arose among members of the Jewish ruling council recorded in Acts 23. When the apostle Paul was being questioned about his belief in the resurrection of Jesus Christ, he stood up and shouted boldly to all the members of that assembly. He told them that he was being called into question because of his hope in the resurrection of the dead. That was a red flag, and a major dispute broke out between the Pharisees and the Sadducees. There was so much confusion and uproar that the Roman commander *"was afraid Paul would be torn to pieces by them."*

Flavius Josephus was a 1st century Jewish historian. His works give an important insight into what life was really like for 1st century Jews. For the Pharisees, the penalty for sin was torment without end, and they stated their belief clearly. In his *Antiquities*, he tells us that the Pharisees

> "believe that souls have an immortal rigor in them, and that under the earth there will be rewards or punishments, according as they have lived virtuously or viciously in this life; and

the latter are to be detained in an everlasting prison."[26]

Elsewhere, he says the Pharisees believe that

"the souls of bad men are subject to eternal punishment."[27]

He further states that another Jewish sect, the Essenes, like the Greeks of their day,

"allot to bad souls a dark and tempestuous den, full of never-ceasing punishments," where they "suffer immortal punishment after their death."[28]

Philo of Alexandria was a Jewish philosopher and a contemporary of Jesus. In a comment about the punishment of Cain who killed his brother Abel, Philo gives another insight into what the conservative Jews at the time of Christ believed.

"Since then the action of this man was a novel one, it was necessary that a novel punishment should be devised for him; and what was it? That he should live continually dying, and that he should in a manner endure an undying and never ending death."[29]

The religious conservatives in Jesus' day clearly believed in endless punishment. However, the words and phrases that *both* Josephus and Philo used to describe what the Pharisees and other groups at the time believed with regard to the fate of the wicked, are *never* found in the New Testament in connection with punishment.

Neither Jesus nor any of the other New Testament writers used the Greek terms translated as everlasting prison, eternal punishment, never-ceasing punishments, immortal punishment after death, and undying and never ending death.

Later, we'll look specifically at what Jesus actually said about after-death punishment to show that the adjective He used really meant *limited duration*. And the noun denoted *suffering resulting in correction*.

For now, I'll simply mention that a major focus of Jesus' ministry was to challenge the teaching of the scribes, Pharisees and teachers of the law. He called them hypocrites, blind guides and snakes because they perverted the true teaching of Scripture for the sake of the tradition handed down to them. When asked by some of these religious leaders why His disciples broke the tradition of the elders, Jesus replied,

> "You hypocrites! Isaiah was right when he prophesied about you: "These people honor me with their lips, but their hearts are far from me. They worship me in vain; their teachings are but rules taught by men."[30]

Jesus was an independent.

A father's care

I shared the following at my dad's funeral.

"To me as a little boy, my father was the greatest man who ever lived! He was firm, but kind. He was wise and understanding. If there was ever a problem, I knew he could handle it.

"One of my first memories of my dad is on a train, going from the village where he had his restaurant, to Chicago. I was three years old.

"He was holding my hand as we walked across what seemed to me to be a dangerous and fearful passageway from one car to another. My dad's hand holding mine was assurance enough that all was well."

Death is most often an unwelcomed guest, leading us

through a dangerous and fearful passageway from this life to the next. But the One who is called Father, abandons no one. Ultimately, everyone will know and understand that in the end, all will be well!

Chapter 4

What did the Early Church teach?

"I hate to say this, George, but it looks like you may have chosen the wrong topic for your research paper. All the books you've consulted so far agree – hell is forever . . . and for a lot of people. In fact, you haven't found anything to even give you hope that your 'hope' may be correct. It looks like you're all alone on this one."

I was sitting at a table in the seminary library when those words went through my mind. They say that people who talk to themselves either have money in the bank, or else they're crazy. I certainly didn't fit the former category, and it was looking more and more like the latter idea might be true.

"Well, let me check the card catalog one more time," I said to myself. *"I can't be the only person in history who ever thought of this . . . or can I?"* That last thought was not particularly encouraging.

This was before card catalogs had been computerized, so I walked over to the large wooden cabinet that housed rows of cards in neat drawers and looked again. I came across another book that seemed to relate directly to the issue at hand.[31]

It was a scholarly work, published exactly 100 years earlier, that specifically addressed the opinions about hell held by the Christian Church throughout its history. I located the book in the stacks and began reading, not expecting to find anything substantially different from what the other books had said.

Then I read the following words in the Preface. Actually, it was *one* word that suddenly leaped off the page!

"The position I have assumed on this point was not anticipated when I began this work. I had adopted the common traditional view, until . . ."

"Until!" What a wonderful word. What a hopeful word!

It signaled that the writer had come across information that had actually changed his mind on the subject. If he no longer held the traditional view, what was his new view? Was it Biblically based? The book was about the history of opinions on the subject of hell. Were there other credible Christians in history who shared this author's different view?

I read the book excitedly and was not disappointed. Yes, the book was Biblically based. Yes, there were other credible Christians in history who shared this author's different view. In fact, some of those others had been leaders in the church. So what was the different view?

It said God would ultimately restore all of His creation.

With new hope, I continued my research. I wrote the paper, turned it in and received an A- for a grade. *"You still don't have money in the bank,"* I whispered to myself. *"But maybe you're not crazy after all!"*

Lessons from history

People are often amazed when they hear that I believe in ultimate restoration.

They've been told all their lives that Christians have always believed in endless punishment, so they think I must be like the proud mother who was watching her son march in a parade. She was thrilled as she watched the marchers passing by. Then she leaned over to her friend and said,

> "Just look at that. Everyone is marching out of step . . . except my son!"

One of the most unexpected discoveries for me as I began reading the history of what Christians have believed about hell, was that endless punishment was *not* the prevailing teaching during the first five centuries after Christ.

This was a critical time in the history of the Church. It was closest to the Apostles. Its influence and impact on the surrounding culture was greater and more effective than at any other time. And its growth was unmatched. And yet, during this time, the doctrine of endless punishment wasn't even a central theme of its message.

Of the six major centers of Christianity in the ancient Church, two – Alexandria and Caesarea – favored the doctrine of ultimate restoration on the principles of *"probably the most important theologian and biblical scholar of the early Greek church"*[82] – a man named Origen.

Two – Antioch and Eastern Syria – favored ultimate restoration on the principles of Theodore of Mopsuestia.

One – Asia Minor, following Irenaeus – held to the annihilation of the wicked.

And only one, Northern Africa – following Tertullian and Augustine – strongly favored the doctrine of future endless punishment.[33]

The Alexandrian School

The city of Alexandria in Egypt was one of the greatest centers of learning in the ancient world.

It was founded by Alexander the Great in c. 331 BC, and became a major center for Greek culture. It was also the home of the largest Jewish community in the world. Alexandria housed the largest library in the ancient world, containing up to 700,000 volumes. It was the first known library of its kind to gather a serious collection of books from beyond its country's borders, and it was at the Library of Alexandria that the scientific method was first conceived and put into practice. It was the center of the world's learning, culture and thought.

Alexandria was also a major center of Christianity.[34] Its significance in the development of the Christian faith can hardly be overestimated. Those who taught had brilliant minds and led exemplary lives.

Over 150 years ago, Charles Kingsley, who was then Regius Professor of Modern History at Cambridge, chaplain to Queen Victoria, private tutor to the future Edward VII, and canon of Westminster, expressed his admiration for this group of early Christians.

"I boldly say that I believe the Alexandrian Christians to have made the best, perhaps the only, attempt yet made by men, to proclaim a true world-philosophy; whereby I mean a philosophy common to all races, ranks, and intellects, embracing the whole phenomena of humanity, and not an arbitrarily small portion of them, and capable of being understood and appreciated by every human being from the highest to the lowest. . . .

"They were enabled to produce, in the lives of millions, generation after generation, a more immense moral improvement than the world had ever seen before. Their disciples did actually become righteous and good men, just in proportion as they were true to the lessons they learnt. They did, for centuries, work a distinct and palpable deliverance on the earth."[35]

So who were these people?

Clement of Alexandria

Clement was a Greek, born in Athens about AD 150, within a couple generations of Jesus and His disciples.

He was very knowledgeable of Greek literature and philosophy, the Old Testament and the gospel of Jesus Christ. He considered it his task to demonstrate to pagans that Christianity was intellectually respectable, and to Christians that Christianity was not only for the uneducated.

People in the ancient world had the same concerns and questions that we have. Like us, they wanted to know what God is really like and what would happen after they died. Is He all-powerful? Or is His power limited like the gods of Greece and Rome? Is He loving? Or does He have the same moody qualities their gods had? What is the final destiny of mankind?

Clement believed that God would ultimately bring about the complete restoration of all His creation. Why? Because God possessed two foundational qualities that lead naturally to that conclusion.

God is *all-powerful*, and He is *loving*. His power corrects, and His love blesses. It is the combination of these qualities that leads to salvation.[36]

Are God's punishments designed primarily to inflict pain on those who have sinned against Him? Clement said, *"No."* God's punishments have a positive purpose. Their goal is to lead people to repentance and salvation.[37]

Does God's patience have a limit? Clement again answered, *"No."* God's work in a person's life doesn't end with physical death. The active power of God is everywhere and always at work, even after we die.[38]

For him, to believe that God is *unable* to save all was unthinkable because that would mean that God is weak. To believe that God is *unwilling* was also unthinkable because that would mean that God is not good. For Clement, God is the Lord of the universe, and He desires the salvation of the universe.

> "For either the Lord does not care for all men; and this is the case either because He is unable (which is not to be thought, for it would be a proof of weakness), or because He is unwilling, which is not the attribute of a good being. . . . Or He does care for all, which is befitting for Him who has become Lord of all. For He is Saviour; not of some, and of others not. . . . For all things are arranged with a view to the salvation of the universe by the Lord of the universe . . ."[39]

Is God like earthly rulers who are primarily concerned with defending their reputations and solidifying their positions? Clement answered, *"No."* God is a Father. As an earthly father chastens his children with a view to correcting them, so we are chastened by our heavenly Father with a view to salvation.

In response to those who thought that God takes vengeance on the wicked, Clement said, *"No."* That could not be the case because that would simply be returning evil for evil. Clement saw God as One who always acts for the good of those He created.

"But as children are chastised by their teacher, or their father, so are we by Providence. But God does not punish, for punishment is retaliation for evil. He chastises, however, for good to those who are chastised, collectively and individually."[40]

For Clement, God's sovereign power coupled with His unfailing love for all, enables Him to ultimately bring about the restoration of all. God never gives up on the sinner.[41]

Origen

The first system of Christian theology was composed and issued by Clement's successor, Origen, around the year AD 230.

Origen was born in Alexandria about AD 185 and died as a martyr at Caesarea not later than AD 251. He was an eminent scholar, the most gifted, most industrious, and most cultivated of all the Early Church fathers. Even heathens and heretics admired or feared his brilliant talent and vast learning. Origen's knowledge embraced all departments of philosophy and theology of his day.[42]

Serious students of the Bible often like to compare various translations to help get a better understanding of the meaning of the actual Biblical text. Origen did the same thing. He compiled an edition of the Old Testament that had six different versions placed side by side for comparison.[43] And he did it by hand, without the benefit of a printing press or the copy function on a personal computer. Prior to St. Augustine, Origen was the most influential theologian of the Christian Church.

One of the fundamental elements of Origen's belief was the doctrine of the ultimate restoration of all fallen beings to their original holiness and union with God.

Like Clement before him, Origen was convinced that the absolute goodness of God, coupled with the persuasive power of His love, would ultimately result in all rational creatures submitting voluntarily to Him through persuasion, not through constraint.[44]

In response to the age-old debate over which is more important in salvation, God's sovereignty or man's freewill, Origen answered, *"Yes!"* Both are vital.

Origen believed that God is able in the course of ages of time to work through people's free will to ultimately bring about their salvation. He does not force submission. God's enemies will be brought into the same kind of heart submission as His apostles and saints.[45]

People have often suggested that the major problem with a belief in restoration is that it doesn't take into account the seriousness of sin. *"You don't understand how much God hates sin!"* they've said. *"He can't stand to have it in His presence."*

Origen would agree . . . and disagree with that position.

Does God hate sin? Absolutely. Will He allow it to continue in His presence? Absolutely not.

But the real question is, "How will God deal with sin?" God isn't going to just pack it up, stick it in a corner of His creation and let it go on forever. Origen saw that God would overcome evil by transforming the evil person – by removing the evil so the person is no longer an enemy.

> "The destruction of the last enemy, indeed, is to be understood, not as if its substance, which was formed by God, is to perish, but because its mind and hostile will, which came not from God, but from itself, are to be destroyed. Its destruction, therefore, will not be its non-existence, but its ceasing to be an enemy . . . For nothing is impossible to the Omnipotent,

nor is anything incapable of restoration to its Creator."[46]

Origen explained that God purifies the soul of its sins as a smelter's oven separates the lead from the gold. This leads to the destruction, not of sinners, but of the *evil* that has filled sinners.

"God consumes as a fire. . . . He enters in as a 'refiner's fire,' to refine the rational nature, which has been filled with the lead of wickedness, and to free it from the other impure materials, which adulterate the natural gold or silver, so to speak, of the soul. And, in like manner, 'rivers of fire' are said to be before God, who will thoroughly cleanse away the evil which is intermingled throughout the whole soul."[47]

If he were alive today, Origen would clearly agree with the comment that God hates sin, but loves the sinner. He had no doubt in his mind that sinners would be punished. But God's purposes for punishment are in keeping with the goodness of His nature.

Elsewhere, Origen used the analogy of a physician.[48] Just as a physician applies methods that sometimes appear severe to the recipient, so God, the Great Physician, works relentlessly in the lives of His created beings to ultimately turn their hearts freely back to Him.

As with Clement, at the heart of Origen's belief was the deep conviction that God loves and desires to save all, along with a fundamental confidence in His ability to carry it out.[49]

Heresy?

Whoa! Hold on a minute. Wasn't Origen condemned as a heretic? And his teaching about restoration declared heresy by the Church centuries ago?

Well, the answer to those questions is a definite yes . . . and no.

Origen was, and is, a very controversial figure. And it's true that both he and his teaching about restoration were at one point condemned as heretical by an early Church council. However, several very important issues surrounding the condemnation seriously call into question its legitimacy.

Origen was a brilliant, energetic and dedicated Christian leader whose positive impact on the development and teaching of the Christian Church was unmatched in his time.

Most of Origen's writings were clearly accepted as orthodox.

Origen's personal life was exemplary. He suffered persecution and even torture for his faith.

And some of his thoughts were speculative. He himself explained that some of his writings were investigations and discussions rather than fixed and certain decisions.[50]

During his life, and for the first couple of hundred years after his death, Origen was considered one of the most important of the Church Fathers, with his writings widely disseminated and used in the Church. Then, three centuries after he died, a Church council in Constantinople condemned him as a heretic, and many of his writings were destroyed.[51]

So what happened to bring about such a tremendous change in attitude? Why did the council declare him a heretic – *300 years* after he was martyred for his faith? Why were others who held similar views never condemned?

These are important, complex questions that many have tried to answer.

The simple answer, and a factor that has played an

important role in many significant events in history, is that politics entered the picture!

The most prominent and influential individual in Church affairs at the time, and the person who initiated the effort to condemn Origen, was not a patriarch. He was not a bishop. He was not even a member of the clergy. He was a politician.

Justinian I, the Eastern Roman Emperor who ruled from AD 527-565, was a strong leader whose ambition was to restore the Roman Empire to its original glory.[52] He saw himself as both king and priest, the supreme head on earth in matters relating to the State and the Church. He ruled with absolute power and did not tolerate dissent, as can be seen by his pronouncement that the emperor's will is law.[53]

Justinian was convinced that the unity of the Empire unconditionally presupposed unity of faith, and those whose beliefs differed from his were subjected to intense persecution. On one occasion in Constantinople, a number of people he deemed as heretics were executed in the Emperor's very presence, some by burning, others by drowning.[54]

As a firm supporter of endless punishment, Justinian pushed hard for the Church to issue a series of judgments against what he called *Origenist* teachings about restoration. But the judgments weren't actually against what Origen wrote and supported. They were against a

> "radicalized . . . doctrine of [restoration] that went far beyond the hopes of Origen or Gregory of Nyssa."[55]

What happened was that the Church council, at Justinian's urging, condemned Origen's name, and blamed him for the radical teaching of others.

There is also a great deal of doubt regarding whether or not the judgments against Origen and his teaching were actually issued by an important *church-wide* council of the Church.[56]

Two series of judgments were issued at the insistence of Justinian. The first was composed of nine articles that he included in a letter to the patriarch Menas in Constantinople in AD 544. These were apparently ratified that year by a *local* council in that city. The second was a list of 15 articles, also issued in the same city of Constantinople.

Some scholars have held that the 15 articles were issued by the Fifth General Council held in Constantinople in AD 553, and that Origen and his teachings about restoration are heretical.

Others, with equally strong credentials, have suggested that there was confusion between the two councils, both held in Constantinople within a nine-year period, and that the judgments against Origen were actually issued by the *local* council in that city in 544. If this is the case, Origen and a distorted view of his belief in ultimate restoration were condemned at a local level, but they were specifically not taken up by the larger and more important church-wide council that met nine years later.[57]

Recent scholarship has suggested that the judgments may have been issued by the assembled bishops of the Fifth General Council, who acknowledged that nothing could be done in the Church contrary to the emperor's will and command,[58] but prior to the actual opening of the convention.[59] If this is true, it would again be the case that the condemnation does not have the clear status of a decision by a church-wide, general council.

What is certain is that the Fifth General Council was called exclusively to deal with a totally separate issue. Nothing whatsoever was said about Origen or Origenism in the call of the Council, nor in any of the letters written in connection with it.

It's also certain that the Council was called by the Eastern Roman Emperor Justinian I rather than the Church leadership. The bishop of Rome, Pope Vigilius, refused to attend it. And the official record of the Council has no mention of the judgments.

Finally, it's certain that the only articles to which Pope Vigilius later agreed, have no mention of the judgments against Origen or his teaching.[60]

The condemnation of Origen was the result of

"vehement and petty personal quarrels ... and a narrow-minded intolerance towards all free speculation."[61]

It brought no gain to the development of Church doctrine, and had a chilling effect on serious religious discussion from that point on.

The editors of the classic, multi-volume set of the writings of the Early Church fathers from AD 100-325 said of Origen,

"The character of Origen is singularly pure and noble; for his moral qualities are as remarkable as his intellectual gifts. The history of the church records the names of few whose patience and meekness under unmerited suffering were more conspicuous than his.

. . . To him belongs the rare honor of convincing heretics of their errors, and of leading them back to the church – a result that must have been due as much to the gentleness and earnestness of his Christian character, as to the prodigious learning, marvelous acuteness, and logical power, which entitle him to be regarded as the greatest of the Fathers."[62]

Gregory of Nyssa

Gregory of Nyssa was a major force in teaching the Deity of Christ that prevailed at the Council of Constantinople in AD 381.

It was there that the Nicene Creed was finally shaped. Gregory actually added the words, *"I believe in the life of the world to come"* to the creed. He died around AD 395 and is still revered as one of the greatest of the Eastern Church fathers.

In AD 787, the Seventh General Council of the Church honored Gregory by naming him, *Father of the Fathers.*[63]

His credentials as an influential leader in the early Christian Church have *never* been questioned, and his position on restoration has *never* been condemned.[64] Reading his comments alone would dispel the notion that the Church has always held to a belief in endless punishment.

Gregory based his belief in the ultimate restoration of all on what he saw as the purpose of punishment, the nature of evil, and the character of God.[65]

Does God punish forever with terrifying pain?

Gregory explained that those who are immature think this and fear it. They are thus motivated to flee from wickedness. However, those with more maturity understand the true purpose of after-death punishment. It's a remedial process instituted by God to ultimately restore to health those who are sick. Like a skilled physician who doesn't stop until his work is finished, God does not give up on those He created.

> "If, however, the soul remains unhealed, the remedy is dispensed in the life that follows this . . . and this to the thoughtless sort is held out as the threat of a terrible correction, in order that through fear of this painful retribution they

may gain the wisdom of fleeing from wickedness: while by those of more intelligence it is believed to be a remedial process ordered by God to bring back man, His peculiar creature, to the grace of his primal condition."[66]

But what about those who have hardened their hearts against God? Is there any hope for them?

Gregory believed that those who had expressed their faith in this life and had humbled themselves before God through baptism did not need any further purification. However, those who would not repent needed to be purified in the succeeding ages by fire.

"But as for those whose weaknesses have become inveterate . . . it is absolutely necessary that they should come to be in something proper to their case – just as the furnace is the proper thing for gold alloyed with dross – in order that, the vice which has been mixed up in them being melted away after long succeeding ages, their nature may be restored pure again to God."[67]

For Gregory, evil is in its nature self-destructive. It will eventually disappear. Because God is good, His ultimate goal is the final accord of the whole universe with Himself.

"In due course evil will pass over into non-existence; it will disappear utterly from the realm of existence. Divine and uncompounded goodness will encompass within itself every rational nature; no single being created by God will fail to achieve the kingdom of God."[68]

What about the powers in the spiritual realm? Is God concerned with that part of His creation, as well? For Gregory, at the heart of God's character is His grace, which reaches even to the angelic world. Not only would the rational creatures on earth be finally restored, but so would those in the spirit world, including *the introducer of evil* – the devil.

> "He accomplished all the results before mentioned, freeing both man from evil, and healing even the introducer of evil himself. For the chastisement, however painful, of moral disease is a healing of its weakness."[69]

Contemporary scholar John R. Sachs concluded his study of the belief in restoration among the early Alexandrian church fathers with the following observation.

> "None of them denied human freedom and responsibility. Each of them at times has rather traditional things to say about eschatological punishment. But what really motivated them was an even stronger conviction about the infinity and incomprehensibility of God's goodness and mercy, revealed and bestowed in the life, death, and resurrection of Christ. There, rather than in the philosophical currents of their times, is where, ultimately, each of these theologians founded his hope that all will be saved."[70]

The School of Antioch

Belief in ultimate restoration was not confined to the Alexandrian Christians.

It was also held by those in Antioch. That city had been founded near the end of the 4th century BC by one of Alexander the Great's generals, and it eventually rivaled Alexandria as the chief city of the Near East. At its peak it had a population of about 500,000 people.

Antioch also became a center of early Christianity.

As the faith was beginning to spread, the Church in

Jerusalem sent Barnabas to Antioch to investigate reports that Greeks in that city had become believers. When he arrived and saw evidence of this, he went on to Tarsus to find Saul, who later became the Apostle Paul. They returned to Antioch together and spent a year meeting and teaching great numbers of people in that city.

Luke, the author of the Gospel of Luke and the Book of Acts, was a native of Antioch. It was in Antioch that the disciples were first called *Christians*.[71]

The city later became a seat of one of the four original patriarchates, along with Jerusalem, Rome, and Alexandria. During the 4th century, Antioch was one of the three most important cities in the Eastern Roman Empire, along with Alexandria and Constantinople.

Diodorus of Tarsus

Diodorus of Tarsus was a Christian bishop and monastic reformer who played a pivotal role in the Council that finalized the Nicene Creed. He died in about AD 390. He was noted for his zeal for the truth, and by all accounts led an exemplary life.[72]

He interpreted the Bible in accordance with its historical context and grammatical structure, and did not allegorize its message. He was the teacher of Theodore of Mopsuestia, and John Chrysostom who was known as one of the greatest preachers in the ancient Church.

Diodorus believed that God's glory is most clearly shown in His loving kindness and mercy – not in punishment. God established after-death punishment as a means of purification for a period of time in order that the greatness of His mercy could ultimately be shown to those He created and loves.

> "For the wicked, also, there are punishments, not perpetual, however, lest the immortality prepared for them should become a

disadvantage; but they are to be tormented for a certain brief period . . . according to the amount of malice in their works.

"They shall, therefore, suffer punishment for a brief space; but immortal blessedness, having no end, awaits them. . . . the punishments to be inflicted for heinous and manifold sins are far more surpassed by the magnitude of mercy. The resurrection, therefore, is regarded as a blessing, not only to the good, but also to the evil."[73]

Theodore of Mopsuestia

Diodorus' student, Theodore, was a bishop in the church for 36 years and was revered at his death.[74] Throughout his long tenure, he enjoyed an excellent reputation for eloquence, learning and orthodoxy.[75] The Nestorian Church conferred on him the title *The Interpreter* because of his merits as one who carefully studied and interpreted the Bible. He was considered the foremost teacher of the school of Antioch.[76]

Theodore's belief in restoration was the direct result of his understanding of the greatness and goodness of God.

Being great, God was not taken by surprise at the entrance of sin into His creation. Being good, He incorporated it into His plan in order to ultimately benefit mankind.

"For since God created man when he did not exist, and made him ruler of so extended a system, and offered so great blessings for his enjoyment, it was impossible that he should have not prevented the entrance of sin, if he had not known that it would be ultimately for his advantage. . ."[77]

54

But how would the entrance of sin into the world benefit those God created?

I'm always amazed at how birds build their nests in the Spring. No one teaches them what to do. They just do it. They build wonderful, often fascinating nests. But all birds of a particular type build the same kind of nest. They are not free to choose what they would like to build. They are programmed, in a sense, to do what they do – and they always do it.

Rational creatures, however, are not like that. We are actually free to do things in different ways.

In his commentary on the Book of Genesis, Theodore explained that the freedom to sin that mankind has is, in itself, a very good thing. God could have made us with instincts like the animals. But He chose to make us free. Theodore understood that created beings left to themselves would surely sin and need to be redeemed. But if they had never been given the freedom to choose evil, they would never truly be able to understand good. In His wisdom, God allowed death to enter the present world so that in the future world His grace would be able to bring life and immortality to all.

> "God divided the creation into two states, the present and the future. In the latter he will bring all to immortality and immutability. In the former he gives us over to death and mutability. For if he had made us at first immortal and immutable, we should not have differed from irrational animals, who do not understand the peculiar characteristics by which they are distinguished.
>
> "For if we had been ignorant of mutability we could not have understood the good of immutability. Ignorant of death, we could not have known the true worth of immortality.

Ignorant of corruption, we could not have properly valued incorruption. Ignorant of the burden of sinful passions, we could not have duly exulted in freedom from such passions. In a word, ignorant of an experiment of evils, we should not have been able properly to understand the opposite forms of good."[78]

Theodore recognized that sin's pleasure is only momentary. In the end, it always leads to sadness. That's why it will never last forever.

". . . the wicked who have committed evil the whole period of their lives, shall be punished till they learn that, by continuing in sin, they only continue in misery. And when, by this means, they shall have been brought to fear God, and to regard Him with good-will, they shall obtain the enjoyment of His grace.[79]

His confidence was ultimately in God's goodness. God is not hard-hearted. He punishes sin. But His punishments have a purpose. And that purpose is for the eventual benefit of the creature.

"God would not revive the wicked at the resurrection, if they must needs suffer only punishment without reformation."[80]

During his lifetime, Theodore was always regarded as a faithful servant of the Church. He was a prominent religious author and was even consulted by distant bishops on important questions. He died in the peace of the Church and at the height of a great reputation.

However, in a situation similar to that of Origen, Theodore was personally condemned *125 years after his death* – at the same General Council of Constantinople called by Justinian I in AD 553.[81] Theodore's belief in ultimate restoration, however, was not condemned at that council.

Other well-known leaders within the Early Church believed in ultimate restoration, or at least did not regard it as a dangerous error.

> "The main Patristic supporters of the [restoration] theory, such as Bardaisan, Clement, Origen, Didymus, St. Anthony, St. Pamphilus Martyr, Methodius, St. Macrina, St. Gregory of Nyssa (and probably the two other Cappadocians), St. Evagrius Ponticus, Diodore of Tarsus, Theodore of Mopsuestia, St. John of Jerusalem, Rufinus, St. Jerome and St. Augustine (at least initially), Cassian, St. Isaac of Nineveh, St. John of Dalyatha, Ps. Dionysius the Areopagite, probably St. Maximus the Confessor, up to John the Scot Eriugena, and many others, grounded their Christian doctrine . . . first of all in the Bible."[82]

Even St. Augustine, the most influential supporter of endless punishment in the Early Church, acknowledged that in his day

> ". . . some – indeed very many – deplore the notion of the eternal punishment of the damned and their interminable and perpetual misery."[83]

Their character and motivation

The prominent defenders of the doctrine of ultimate restoration were strong believers in the divinity of Christ, the Trinity, the incarnation and the atonement, and the doctrine of regeneration. They were exemplary in their personal piety, their devotion to Christ, their Christian activity, and their missionary zeal, as well as their learning and intellectual power and accomplishments. In fact, they were greatly superior in these areas to many who condemned them in later ages.[84]

This teaching was strongest in the Greek-speaking portion of the Church where the language of the New Testament was a living tongue. It was strongest in the Church's greatest era of growth and impact. And it declined as the Church's purity declined.

The traditional view of endless punishment, on the other hand, was strongest where the New Testament was less read in its original language and during the most corrupt ages of the Church.[85]

Clement of Alexandria, Origen, Gregory of Nyssa, Diodorus of Tarsus, Theodore of Mopsuestia and others saw God as One who desires the salvation of all, and is wise enough and powerful enough to accomplish what He desires.

J. W. Hanson, a strong supporter of restoration in the 19th century made a very insightful observation about the motivation of many in the early Christian Church who believed that God would ultimately restore all.

> "The talismatic word of the Alexandrian fathers, as of the New Testament, was FATHER. This word, as now, unlocked all mysteries, solved all problems, and explained all the enigmas of time and eternity. Holding God as Father, punishment was held to be remedial, and therefore restorative, and final recovery from sin universal. . . . For centuries in Christendom after the Alexandrine form of Christianity had waned, the Fatherhood of God was a lost truth, and most of the worst errors of the modern creeds are due to that single fact, more than to all other causes."[86]

A theological question

"I wonder what he'll say," I asked myself as I walked into his office. *"I certainly don't think my paper will have*

convinced him to change his mind about the afterlife. After all, it's a preliminary study written by a student. But I hope it will give him reason to consider looking into the issue further."

The man I was talking about was a well-respected New Testament scholar who had been my adviser at the seminary for the previous three years. He had always shown a sincere interest in his students, and I had felt free to ask him to read my research paper to see what he thought.

"I read your paper, George," he said. *"And I have to say, in all honestly, that it does not fit in with my theology. However, if it is any encouragement to you, I'm convinced that God is bigger than my theology."*

His words did encourage me. *"Someday,"* I thought, *"I'll have to look into this issue in more depth."*

"Who knows? Maybe I'll even write a book!"

Chapter 5

What do the ancient creeds tell us?

"What's the matter, George? Is anything wrong?" my wife asked as I hung up the phone. *"I'm not sure,"* I answered.

The call had been from the chairman of the board that oversaw the church we had been members of for 20 years.

He was a friend who asked if we could meet later that night at Starbucks to talk. He didn't mention what he wanted to talk about, but I was pretty sure it had something to do with my book. I had given a copy of an earlier version of the manuscript to one of the pastors a couple of months earlier. He, in turn, had spoken to the elders about it.

"To tell you the truth," he said as we sat down later that night, *"I honestly don't know what to do. You and your family have been actively involved in the church for a long time. We served on the elder board together a number of years ago. People respect you a lot.*

"As you can imagine, the board had an interesting and

lively discussion about you and your views at one of our meetings. Since your book hasn't been published yet, we figured we had some time before we needed to make a definite decision about what to do.

"Unfortunately, that is no longer the case. We just received a letter from a member asking us how we can continue to allow you to stay a member when your belief clearly disagrees with the church's Statement of Faith."

We talked for a while. I answered his questions about what I actually believed about the nature and duration of hell, and how I came to my conclusions. I assured him that I was not interested in being the cause of any kind of division within the church.

"Ideas have consequences," I said. *"I knew when I began to write my book that something like this was bound to happen. I decided at the time that I was willing to accept the consequences. Let me talk this over with my wife, and I'll get back to you on what we think we should do."*

Major change is almost always difficult.

But, when the change means stepping away from people and organizations that have been a significant part of your life for a very long time, it's especially hard. This was one more time when I was so very, very grateful for the wife God had given me.

We talked over the situation. We prayed together. And we agreed on what was clearly the right thing to do. We would quietly leave the church.

True Christianity

What does it mean to be *Christian*?

There are many individuals and groups throughout the world who claim that title but differ significantly from others who claim the same thing. In fact, according to the Center for the Study of Global Christianity at Gordon-Conwell

Theological Seminary, there are currently an estimated 45,000 different Christian denominations in the world.[87]

Some who claim the mantle of Christianity meet in large buildings that are beautifully adorned with gold, fine wood and massive stone work. Others who make the same claim meet in houses or under a tree.

Some who claim to be Christians use a variety of electronic and acoustic musical instruments to sing contemporary songs with their arms waving in the air. Others who claim the name Christian use no instrumentation at all, sit quietly and only sing the Psalms.

Some who say they are Christians wash one another's feet . . . or speak in tongues . . . or claim to have the gift of healing or prophecy or wisdom. Others do none of these things.

Most who claim the name Christian meet together with like minded people on Sunday for a time of worship. Others meet on Saturday, and some on Friday.

Some who claim to be Christian baptize infants. Others baptize only adults.

Some have communion or "share the Eucharist" every time they meet. Others do so only once a month. Or once a year.

If you ask Baptists or Presbyterians if they're Christians, they'll say, *"Yes."* If you ask Roman Catholics if they're Christians, they'll say, *"Yes."* If you ask Anglicans or members of the Eastern Orthodox Church or people who attend services at a Charismatic, Pentecostal, Independent Bible or Seventh Day Adventist church if they're Christians, they'll all answer, *"Yes."*

However, many in each of those groups would say that the others are not.

So what does it really mean to be Christian?

Statements of faith

Most churches, organizations or groups today that call themselves Christian have some kind of statement of faith to let people know their core beliefs about who God is, who Jesus Christ is, who the Holy Spirit is, what they believe about the Bible, the rules governing their church, and their specific worship practices.

The primary purpose of these statements is to let those outside the faith know what they, as Christians, believe.

A secondary purpose is to make other Christians aware of their distinctive positions on various issues so they can find a place to worship together with like-minded individuals.

Unfortunately, these statements of faith often prevent unity by separating one group of Christian believers from others who do not share their views. Sometimes those who disagree are considered untaught or mistaken. Sometimes they are considered heretics whose views must be eliminated, and those who promote them silenced.

Most people are unaware that a document actually exists that was agreed upon by leaders from the entire Christian Church who gathered together for the specific purpose of defining what was essential to believe in order to be considered truly Christian.

And interestingly, the council that issued it specifically prohibited other creeds (statements of faith) from being formulated and presented as the official teaching of the Christian Church.[88]

That document is known as the Nicene Creed.

It was originally drafted at the Council of Nicea in AD 325, with later modifications made at the Council of Constantinople in AD 381. It's a statement of faith accepted by almost all those who claim to be Christians, even today.

In addition to the Nicene Creed, the Apostles Creed which preceded it has generally been accepted by all those in the East and West who call themselves Christians.

Most committed Christians would have no hesitation whatsoever in declaring that these two creeds contain what they believe is the heart of their faith. In fact, many of these same Christians actually recite them on a regular basis in their worship services as part of their declaration of what we, as Christians, believe.

Another great surprise for me when I began to look into the issue of after-death punishment was that those ancient statements of faith do not contain a hint of the doctrine of endless punishment.

The reason, of course, is that it was not considered an important tenet of the faith at that time, and there were a great many believers who did not subscribe to it.

The Apostles' Creed

The Apostles' Creed is the oldest existing authorized declaration of the Christian faith in the shape of a creed.

Scholars agree that it was not written by the New Testament apostles, even though it carries that title.[89] It does, however, contain a concise description of what the Early Church believed was important to emphasize.

One highly regarded historian wrote the following about the significance of the Creed over 100 years ago.

> "As the Lord's Prayer is the Prayer of prayers, the Decalogue the Law of laws, so the Apostles' Creed is the Creed of creeds. It contains all the fundamental articles of the Christian faith necessary to salvation, in the form of facts, in simple Scripture language, and in the most natural order – the order of revelation . . . It is by far the best popular

summary of the Christian faith ever made within so brief a space."[90]

As printed here, the portion in regular type was probably written in the early or middle part of the 2nd century and was in Greek. The portion in italic was added later by the Western Church, and was in Latin.

> "I believe in God the Father Almighty *maker of heaven and earth*, and in Jesus Christ his only son our Lord, who was *conceived* by the Holy Ghost, born of the Virgin Mary, suffered under Pontius Pilate, was crucified, *dead,* and buried. *He descended into hell.* The third day he arose again from the dead; he ascended into heaven and sitteth at the right hand of *God* the Father *Almighty.* From thence he shall come to judge the quick and the dead. I believe in the Holy Ghost, the Holy *Catholic* Church; *the communion of saints*, the forgiveness of sins, the resurrection of the body, *and the life everlasting.* Amen."[91]

The creed tells us that Christ *"descended into hell,"* but says nothing about His purpose for doing that.

It says that Christ will one day *"judge the quick and the dead,"* but nothing is mentioned about the nature or duration of that judgment.

The creed speaks of the *"resurrection of the body,"* and the later form mentions *"the life everlasting."*

But not a word is written about the endless, conscious suffering of the wicked.

That belief was not included in the Creed because it was not universally held and taught by those who were leaders in the Church at that time. It was also not considered an essential tenet of the faith at a time when Christianity was first being introduced to the pagan world around it, and when it was making its greatest impact.

The Nicene Creed

The next oldest creed, and the only one officially authorized by a consensus of the entire Christian Church, is the Nicene Creed.

It's a statement of faith accepted by almost all those who claim to be Christians in the Roman Catholic Church, the Eastern Orthodox Churches, the Assyrian Church of the East, the Oriental Orthodox Churches, and almost all of the Protestant churches, including the Lutheran Church, the Anglican Communion, the Reformed Churches, the Presbyterian Church, the Congregationalist Churches, most Baptist Churches and the Methodist Church.

Like the Apostles' Creed before it, the Nicene Creed says nothing at all about endless punishment. Eternal hell was professed by a portion of the Christian Church at the time, but it was not believed by enough people to be included.

The portion of the Creed printed here in regular type was composed at Nicea in AD 325. The portion in italic was added in AD 381 at the Council of Constantinople.

"We believe in one God, the FATHER Almighty, Maker of *heaven and earth, and of* all things visible and invisible.

"And in one Lord JESUS CHRIST, the *only-begotten* Son of God, begotten of the Father *before all worlds*,[92] Light of Light, very God of very God, begotten, not made, being of one substance with the Father; by whom all things were made; who for us men, and for our salvation, came down *from heaven*, and was incarnate *by the Holy Ghost of the Virgin Mary*, and was made man; he *was crucified for us under Pontius Pilate, and suffered, and was buried,* and the third day he rose again, *according to the Scriptures,* and ascended into heaven, *and sitteth on the right hand of the Father,* from thence he shall come *again, with glory,* to judge the quick and the dead; *whose kingdom shall have no end.*

"And in the HOLY GHOST, *the Lord and Giver of life, who proceedeth from the Father,[93] who with the Father and the Son together is worshiped and glorified, who spake by the prophets. In one holy catholic and apostolic Church; we acknowledge one baptism for the remission of sins; we look for the resurrection of the dead, and the life of the world to come. Amen."[94]*

As with the Apostles' Creed before it, the Nicene Creed talks of judgment for those who are living and those who are dead. It talks of the resurrection of the dead and the life of the world to come, but not a word is written in this clear statement of faith about the nature or duration of after-death punishment.

None of the four great General Councils held in the first four centuries of the Christian era – those at Nicea, Constantinople, Ephesus and Chalcedon – condemned the belief in ultimate restoration or even mentioned endless punishment as the consensus belief of the Church, although both doctrines were held by various key participants at the time.

As noted earlier, a radicalized version of Origen's doctrine of ultimate restoration was for the first time condemned at a local council in Constantinople in AD 544, and, possibly, prior to the General Council of Constantinople held nine years later in AD 553.

However, the belief actually taught by Clement, Origen,

Gregory of Nyssa, Theodore of Mopsuestia, and others was not condemned at that Council, and has never been formally condemned in any general council of the Church.

The Definition of Chalcedon

The Definition of Chalcedon was adopted at the Council of Chalcedon in AD 451.

It's not a creed, but rather a clarification and expansion of the belief that the Son is truly God and truly man.

The Council of Chalcedon is one of the general councils accepted by the Eastern Orthodox, Roman Catholic and many Protestant churches. But it's the first council not recognized by the Oriental Orthodox churches.

Nothing whatsoever is mentioned in this statement about the ultimate destinies of mankind.

The Athanasian Creed

The first statement of belief to mention anything about endless punishment is what has come to be known as the Athanasian Creed.[95]

It's really an early catechism. And unlike the Apostles Creed and the Nicene Creed, it includes a solemn declaration at the beginning and at the end that those who reject it will be lost forever. It was used for a time in the Western churches but has never been accepted by the Eastern Church.

The name attributes this creed to Athanasius, who was one of the strongest proponents of the Deity of Christ at the Council of Nicea. However, since the middle of the 17th century, it has been determined that Athanasius did not write it or even know of its existence.

It was most likely written in the 6th century in Latin, while Athanasius lived in the 4th century and wrote in Greek.

It's not found in any of the genuine writings of Athanasius, and none of his contemporaries ever mention it.

There is no mention of it in any of the records of the General Councils, and it addresses theological concerns generally taken to reflect Augustinian theology that developed after Athanasius died. It was first attributed to Athanasius in the 9th century in the West, but was unknown in the East until the 11th century where it was either rejected or modified.

> "The damnatory clauses, especially when sung or chanted in public worship, grate harshly . . . and it may well be doubted whether they are consistent with true Christian charity and humility, and whether they do not transcend the legitimate authority of the Church."[96]

The Nicene Creed is the true Statement of Faith of the Christian church.

The distinctions spelled out in the various other statements that churches and organizations have drawn up since then are real and held strongly by their worshippers. However, perhaps it would be better if we called them Statements of Distinctives.

Ideas and consequences

"Dear Overseeing Board:

"When Suzan and I applied for membership, I gave a copy of my paper to the pastor and spoke to him about what I thought. He, in turn, spoke to the elders. Because my belief in ultimate restoration was a private hope for me at the time, and not a settled conviction, the decision was made that we would be able to join the church.

"About 4 years ago, I decided to revisit the topic to look into the issue in much more depth. I have since written a book on the subject, and what had been a private hope has now become a settled conviction.

"Because that belief clearly does not agree with the church's Statement of Faith, Suzan and I have decided it would be best if we withdrew our membership. We want to be true to our vows, and do not want to be the cause of any kind of division within the church, especially at this critical time of transition.

"Please accept this letter as our request to have our names removed from the list of members.

"We are very grateful for our time at the church. It has played a wonderful role in our family and been a great blessing to us.

"May God richly bless you as the overseeing board, and the church in general, as you seek to honor Him in the days ahead."

Chapter 6

What happened in the Middle Ages?

It was clearly the right time, but it was *not* something I looked forward to.

The bulk of my research had been completed. I had written and revised my manuscript more than once. And a ministry I had been working with for several years was about to break for the summer.

A prominent Christian leader had unexpectedly published a book a couple of months earlier that touched on the issue of universal salvation.[97] That book created an immediate controversy within the Christian community and quickly became a national best seller. It was even the subject of the cover story for an issue of TIME magazine.[98] What had been a marginal topic that most Christians ignored, suddenly became a topic everyone was talking about.

Before I could speak openly about what I thought, I needed to make my views known to the person who headed up the ministry.

"I wanted to make you aware of a manuscript of a book that I've written on the issue of ultimate destinies," I wrote in an email.

"It is written from a clearly Biblical and theologically conservative perspective. However, my conclusion is that the traditionally held belief in the conscious, endless punishment of the wicked is not the true teaching of Scripture. Rather, the book argues that God will ultimately restore all of His creation to its initial perfection.

"Because this differs from the ministry's statement of faith, and I cannot continue to hold the view only in private, I wanted to pass along a copy of the manuscript so you can see what I have actually written."

I expected this to come as quite a shock, and I was right!

"I am devastated by the word you have given me regarding your very clear departure from biblical teaching (I know you do not view it as that)," he wrote back, *"and I have had difficulty sleeping some because of my love and concern for you and for the unintended consequences of the action you are taking in going public with your beliefs in this matter.*

I started to read your manuscript, and before I got to the end of the introduction, a heaviness of spirit came on me, one so burdensome I could not read beyond that point. . . . I do not think you have any idea of the serious potential consequences of your beliefs and of going public with your views."

We spoke a few days later, after which a message was sent to others involved in the ministry.

They were informed that

"George Sarris has been terminated for departure from the ministry Statement of Faith . . . We are deeply grieved by the turn of events which has necessitated this decision

and greatly concerned about where his doctrinal aberrations are taking him."

The die had been cast.

A question of power

If what you've read so far makes sense, then a major question looms before us.

"What on earth happened?"

If belief in ultimate restoration was prominent in the early centuries of the Christian Church, why did it go out of favor to the point of being considered heresy in the Middle Ages?

If belief in endless punishment was not the prevailing view in the Early Church, why did it rise to such a dominant position in later centuries?

Good questions!

Karl Marx said, *"Religion is the opiate of the people."* Jesus said, *"The truth shall set you free."* Religion enslaves. Truth liberates. Political and ecclesiastical rulers throughout history have generally understood just how true these concepts are and have acted accordingly.[99]

The great transition from the vibrant Christianity of the first few centuries after Christ to the harsh, monolithic structure of the Middle Ages began with the conversion of the Roman Emperor Constantine. In AD 313, he issued the *Edict of Milan* which legalized Christianity in the empire and ended the persecution of Christians.

He supported the Church financially, built large churches, exempted the clergy from paying taxes, promoted Christians to high office, and returned confiscated property taken during the persecutions under the Emperor Diocletian. Because of his support, Christianity quickly became the dominant and semi-official religion of Rome.

As Christianity grew in influence, the spiritually powerful

Early Church quickly became the materially powerful *Imperial Church.*

Christian leaders were increasingly tempted to please the state and guard their positions rather than seek the truth. Rome grew in power and influence over the former centers of Christianity in Alexandria, Palestine and the Eastern cities. And the Bible increasingly came to be read in its Latin translations rather than in the original Greek and Hebrew.

The bishop of Rome took on the title *Pontifex Maximus,* originally used by the Roman Emperors in their role as high priest of the Roman pantheon, and claimed supremacy over the other bishops.[100]

What the Church gained in material power, however, it lost in moral force and independence.

Once favors began to be granted, Church discipline and commitment began to decline as those with mixed motives attained positions of leadership. The greatest casualty of this increased influence of the State in the affairs of the Church, was the end of freedom – freedom of thought and freedom of inquiry.

The use of force to punish heretics quickly became the rule.[101] A heretic was one who didn't hold the orthodox view. And the orthodox view became whatever those currently in power determined it to be.

Power corrupts, and absolute power corrupts absolutely.

Examples of this have been seen countless times throughout history in monarchies and dictatorships where despots punished enemies to gain and retain power. However, the power to punish only on earth has its limitations. But how about adding the concept of never-ending punishment in the afterlife? That is real power! And an irresistible temptation for many who desired supreme control over all others.

The grasp for power accelerated under Emperor Justinian I in the 6th century, fueled in part by the writings of one of the most influential of the Latin fathers.

St. Augustine

The most brilliant and influential theologian after Origen was Aurelius Augustinus, known to us as St. Augustine.

He was born in what is now Algeria in AD 354 and died in 430. He converted to Christianity at the age of 33. He's one of the most important and influential figures in the development of Western Christianity, as well as the history of Western thought.[102] The list of his works consists of more than 100 separate titles. It was Augustine who said,

> "Thou hast made us for Thyself and our hearts are restless till they rest in Thee."[103]

Augustine lived as a pagan intellectual during his early years and followed the Manichean religion. According to the beliefs of the Manicheans, there exists a dualism in the universe with good and evil eternally at war with each other. After his conversion to Christ, some of that thinking may have influenced his view of ultimate destinies.

Learning a foreign language is not easy, especially if you don't like your teacher.

That's not only true today; it was also true in the past . . . and it was true for Augustine. The classical schooling he received in colonial North Africa was conducted principally in Latin.

As a boy he rebelled against learning Greek because he didn't like the Greek literature he was forced to study, and his teachers beat their students. He commented in his *Confessions*,

> "But why did I so much hate the Greek, which I studied as a boy? I do not yet fully know . . .

For not one word of it did I understand, and to
make me understand I was urged vehemently
with cruel threats and punishments."[104]

The result was that Augustine couldn't read the New
Testament in its original language. That put him at a clear
disadvantage in understanding some of the finer points of
the Greek text, as compared with the earlier Greek fathers
who read the New Testament in their native tongue.[105]

Unlike Clement, Origen, Gregory of Nyssa, Diodorus,
Theodore of Mopsuestia and others who understood the
Greek term defining the duration of punishment as meaning
an indeterminate period of time, Augustine assumed and
insisted that it meant never-ending. We'll look carefully at
the meaning of this term – *aion* – in chapter 10.

In contrast to those who saw God's sovereign power and
divine love working together even after death to accomplish
the salvation of all, Augustine believed that most would
never be saved.

"But many more are left under punishment than
are delivered from it, in order that it may thus be
shown what was due to all."[106]

When presented with the dilemma of whether God *would*
save all but *couldn't* – which would place a limit on His
power. Or that He *could* save all but *wouldn't* – which
would place a limit on His love. Augustine chose the latter.

He was convinced that God is sovereign and could save
all. But in fact, He will only save some. In response to the
accusation that this would mean that God is not loving,
Augustine explained that all deserve to suffer endlessly.
God's decision to save some who clearly don't deserve
salvation is evidence that He is not uncaring.[107]

In Augustine's view, God does not have a kind purpose in
punishing because God has so structured the next world
that death will never be abolished.

". . . although it be true that in this world there is no flesh which can suffer pain and yet cannot die, yet in the world to come there shall be flesh such as now there is not, as there will also be death such as now there is not. For death will not be abolished, but will be eternal, since the soul will neither be able to enjoy God and live, nor to die and escape the pains of the body. The first death drives the soul from the body against her will: the second death holds the soul in the body against her will. The two have this in common, that the soul suffers against her will what her own body inflicts."[108]

Although he originally taught that heretics shouldn't be forced to believe, Augustine later changed his mind. He argued that the punishment of heretics is a form of charity, motivated by the Church's desire to heal. Heretics and schismatics should be compelled through fear or pain to return to the Church where they would later be influenced by teaching.

"For many have found advantage (as we have proved, and are daily proving by actual experiment), in being first compelled by fear or pain, so that they might afterwards be influenced by teaching . . . But while those are better who are guided aright by love, those are certainly more numerous who are corrected by fear . . . many must first be recalled to their Lord by the stripes of temporal scourging, like evil slaves, and in some degree like good-for-nothing fugitives."[109]

With the power of the state behind a doctrine that deemed it right and necessary to punish heretics, a principle was set in place which resulted in horrific consequences.[110]

The persecuted minority

Belief in ultimate restoration was considered heretical by the Church of the Middle Ages and vigorously opposed and punished. But even in the midst of tremendous persecution, the belief that God was good and would bring about the complete restoration of all His creation was never a lost hope.

Maximus the Confessor was a Greek monk of the 7th century who held this view, although he was careful to talk of it only with those who were mature in the faith.[111] He is venerated as a saint in both Eastern and Western Christianity. His title of *Confessor* means that he suffered for the Christian faith, but wasn't directly martyred. Maximus believed that at the end of the age, God's grace would transform and renew the entire human race.[112]

Saint Isaac of Nineveh, a 7th century holy man, is considered one of the greatest theologians of the Eastern Orthodox tradition. When his writings were translated into several European languages, his name became known and appreciated also in the West. Isaac believed that God is both sovereign and good.

"It is not the way of the compassionate Maker to create rational beings in order to deliver them over mercilessly to unending affliction in punishment for things of which He knew even before they were fashioned, aware how they would turn out when He created them – and whom nonetheless He created. . . . All kinds and manner of chastisements and punishments that come from Him are not brought about in order to requite past actions, but for the sake of the subsequent gain to be gotten in them . . . This is what the Scriptures bring to our attention and remind us of . . . that God is not one who requites evil, but He sets aright evil."[113]

In the 8th century in the West, Clement of Ireland was deposed from the priesthood for teaching that when Christ descended into hell, He restored all the damned.

In the 9th, John Scotus Erigena, an Irishman and noted Greek scholar, believed in ultimate restoration.

In the 11th century, the Albigenses held the doctrine.

In the 12th, Raynold, Abbot of St. Martin's in France, was charged before a council with holding *"that all men will eventually be saved."*

In the 13th century, Solomon, Bishop of Bassorah, affirmed universal salvation.

The Lollards in the 14th century taught the doctrine in Bohemia and Austria.

In the early 15th century, a sect called *Men of Understanding* taught it in Flanders, as did Tauler of Strasbourg and John Wessel, who, with others, have been called *the Reformers before the Reformation.*[114]

The belief was also found as one of the 900 theses which scholar Giovanni Pico della Mirandola proposed to defend in public debate in Rome in 1487. He said,

> "A mortal sin of finite duration is not deserving
> of eternal but only of temporal punishment."[115]

It was among the theses pronounced heretical by Pope Innocent VIII in his bull of August 4, 1484, and the debate was never held.

Christians today often look with disdain on the Islamic world for not allowing a Muslim to question the teaching of clerics or change faith without facing punishment and, possibly, death.

During most of the Middle Ages, and even through the Reformation and up to modern times, that was the position of most of Christendom. To question or oppose the teaching of those in authority meant persecution, torture and sometimes death.

Not interested

"I'm not surprised," I said to a friend who was concerned about my letter of termination.

"It's very difficult for someone in his position to seriously consider changing his view on hell. If he did, he'd have to resign from his position and leave his denomination."

My friend had expressed an interest in my manuscript and had asked his pastor if he would be willing to read it. The pastor had said yes, but after receiving a copy, made a casual remark about it being heretical and said he wasn't interested.

The pastor was a prominent and well-known member of his denomination.

My friend felt bad.

Chapter 7

What happened from then to now?

Looking back, it was one of the most important days in all my years of research on God's ultimate plan for all of us.

I could hardly believe my eyes.

I had been searching the internet to see if I could find a copy of the book that had first given me hope for ultimate restoration.[116] It had been published in 1878, but I thought, *"Who knows? Maybe I can find a copy somewhere."*

My search led me to a website, and as I read, I was both stunned and amazed.

For the previous 29 years, I thought I was the only contemporary, Biblically focused Christian who believed that hell was *not* forever. Suddenly, I was looking at a website operated by people who believed the same thing.[117]

I located a telephone number and made a call.

"Hi, my name is George Sarris. Do you have time to talk

for a few minutes?" I briefly shared my experience and asked, *"Do you actually believe the Bible teaches that hell is temporary, and that all mankind will eventually get into heaven?"*

His answer was simple, *"Yes!"*

We talked for quite a while. He told me how he had come to his belief, and suggested some additional resources I could look at.

I hung up the phone and sat back in my chair. I had found an ally. Another person who was convinced that the Bible, *correctly translated*, proves Jesus Christ is the Savior of all mankind, loser of none.[118]

I found out something else that day, something that to me was even more exciting! Something that didn't exist when I wrote my research paper.

I discovered that the *internet* offered access to information that previously could only be found in a theological library. As I sat in front of my computer, I realized there were search engines to put me in contact with many websites. The internet provided a treasure trove of documents, books and articles from around the world that I could never have accessed before!

I felt like the proverbial kid in a candy store. I felt like I was about to embark on an exciting journey.

And I did!

Searching for truth

Experience certainly confirms the old saying,

> *you can fool all the people some of the time, and some of the people all the time, but you cannot fool all the people all the time.*

Eventually, truth always rises to the surface. It's often attacked, persecuted and defamed, but it can never be totally blotted out. Why? Because truth is the only thing that's consistent with reality.

When Martin Luther posted his 95 Theses on the door of Castle Church in Wittenberg, Germany on October 31, 1517, he had no intention of leaving the Roman Catholic Church or establishing another church.

His plan was simply to debate a number of issues in an attempt to get to the truth, and reform what he saw as doctrinal and ecclesiastical errors. His action, however, was the match that quickly started a church reformation fire in the West that engulfed much of Europe and then North America.

The goal of the Reformers was to get back to the faith and power of early Christianity. Some of their changes may have gone too far. Some, not far enough. It was in this climate of seeking truth that the belief in ultimate restoration began to surface once again. It was still regarded as heresy by most people in the Protestant Reformation churches, but certain groups and individuals began to consider it.

Groups and individuals in Europe

The view that God's goodness would ultimately prevail in all of His creation was allowed as a private, charitable hope in the Lutheran Church of Germany.

Martin Luther wrote in a letter to Hansen von Rechenbert in 1522,

> "God forbid that I should limit the time for acquiring faith to the present life. In the depths of the divine mercy there may be opportunity to win it in the future state."[119]

The Anabaptists were a large and varied group of Christians that sprang up in Switzerland and Germany. They got their name because they rejected infant baptism, believing that only adults who understood their faith should be baptized.

Many also held to a belief in ultimate restoration and were severely persecuted by the other reformation churches for holding that view. According to Article XVII of the Lutheran Augsburg Confession of 1530,

> "They condemn the Anabaptists, who think that there will be an end to the punishments of condemned men and devils."[120]

The Moravians were followers of Jan Hus, the Czech reformer who was burned at the stake in 1415. Some members of this group believed that all would ultimately be saved. One of them, Peter Boehler (1712-1775), went as a missionary from Europe to the American colonies of Georgia and South Carolina, and later led a group of Moravians to Pennsylvania where they founded the towns of Nazareth and Bethlehem. He wrote that

> ". . . all the damned souls shall yet be brought out of hell."[121]

Many Quakers in England and later in the United States also held this view, along with groups within the Mennonite, Amish and Brethren communities.

When the Protestants in England drew up their Forty-two Articles of Religion in 1553, ultimate restoration was condemned. However, 10 years later when the doctrines of the church were revised, the number of articles was reduced to 39. Included in those dropped was Article 42, the article that condemned the belief that all men would eventually be saved.[122]

Since that time, ultimate restoration has not been a forbidden doctrine in the Church of England.

William Law

William Law (1686-1761) was an Anglican priest who

influenced John Wesley and others active in the evangelical revival in 18th century England.

He was one of those rare individuals in history who was willing to do the right thing, regardless of the negative consequences that may result from that decision. When his conscience wouldn't allow him to take the oaths of allegiance to the new government of George I, he gave up his position at Emmanuel College, Cambridge.

Like the early Greek Fathers, Law saw God's never-ending love and unlimited power working together to bring about the restoration of all things. In an address to his fellow clergy, he explained what he saw as the working of God throughout the ages.

> "The love that brought forth the existence of all things, changes not through the fall of its creatures, but is continually at work, to bring back all fallen nature and creature to their first state of goodness. . . . God creating, God illuminating, God sanctifying, God threatening and punishing, God forgiving and redeeming, is but one and the same essential, immutable, never ceasing working of the divine nature."[123]

Andrew Jukes

Andrew Jukes (1815-1901) was a Deacon in the Church of England, and later became part of the Plymouth Brethren. He baptized Hudson Taylor, founder of the China Inland Mission, in the Hull Brethren Assembly in 1852. To this day, Taylor is the best-known and one of the most highly respected Protestant missionaries to China.

It was Jukes' conviction that those who are the first to experience salvation will not experience it alone. Rather, they would become the means by which others would also come to know God's grace and goodness. God doesn't end His work of grace when a person dies. He continues to work through the ages to bring each person to repentance and humility.[124]

> "But all the saved have once been lost . . . The fact therefore that of these lost some are lost for a longer or a shorter period, proves nothing against their final restoration; for the Good Shepherd must 'go after that which is lost, until He find it.'"[125]

George MacDonald

George MacDonald (1824-1905) was a Scottish author, poet and Christian minister. He's not as well-known as C. S. Lewis or J. R. R Tolkien, but his fairy tales and fantasy novels greatly influenced those later writers.

In fact, the major character in Lewis' *The Great Divorce* is named George MacDonald. Lewis so admired him that he published a book of extracts from MacDonald's writings. In the Introduction to *George MacDonald: An Anthology*, Lewis wrote:

> "This collection, as I have said, was designed not to revive MacDonald's literary reputation but to spread his religious teaching . . . I know hardly any other writer who seems to be closer, or more continually close, to the Spirit of Christ Himself . . . I have never concealed the fact that I regarded him as my master; indeed I fancy I have never written a book in which I did not quote from him."[126]

MacDonald was convinced that God's intent is to bring about a complete victory over sin and death not simply by punishing sin, but by destroying it. God's punishments have a positive purpose. The reason behind suffering in hell is to bring deliverance.

> "Primarily, God is not bound to punish sin; he is bound to destroy sin . . . The only vengeance worth having on sin is to make the sinner himself its executioner . . . the opposite of evil is good, not suffering; the opposite of sin is not suffering, but righteousness. The path across the gulf that divides right from wrong is not the fire, but repentance . . . It is a deliverance into the pure air of God's ways of thinking and feeling."[127]

F. W. Farrar

Frederick W. Farrar (1831-1903) was an Anglican writer and preacher. He became successively Canon of Westminster, Archdeacon of Westminster, and Dean of Canterbury.

In a series of sermons preached in Westminster Abbey in 1877, Farrar greatly surprised his audience by speaking about the possibility that God might, in His grace, ultimately save all. He later wrote an extensive defense of his views with the following concluding comment.

> "For, according to the Scriptures, though I know not what its nature will be or how it will be effected, I believe in the restitution of all things; and I believe in the coming of that time when – though in what sense I cannot pretend to explain or to fathom – GOD WILL BE ALL IN ALL."[128]

Individuals and groups in America

If you walk down the streets of Tokyo, almost everyone you meet was born in Japan. If you walk down the streets of Paris, the vast majority of people were born in France. If you walk down the streets of Mumbai, almost everyone you come in contact with was born in India. But if you walk down the streets of New York City, I'm told that about a third of those who live there are first generation immigrants who were born outside the U.S.

The American Colonies were initially settled by British, French, German, Dutch and other European immigrants, many of whom had been persecuted severely back in their homelands. Although most were Christians, they differed greatly in their beliefs.

As a result, religious tolerance was viewed as an extremely important virtue and became a central tenet of the U.S. Constitution. A number of prominent Americans believed in the ultimate restoration of all.

> "In America before the time of organized Universalism there were many representatives of this faith: Sir Henry Vane Jr., and other mystics; the German Baptists . . . some of the Moravians; several Episcopalians, especially William Smith, founder of the University of Pennsylvania, and for many years president of the general convention of the Protestant Episcopal Church; several leading Congregationalists, including Charles Chauncey and Jonathan Mayhew."[129]

Charles Chauncy

Charles Chauncy (1705-1787) was a Congregationalist minister in Boston. He was educated at Harvard and ordained as a minister of the First Church in Boston in 1727 where he remained for 60 years.

He was an intellectual who strongly opposed the emotional revivalism of the Great Awakening. Next to

Jonathan Edwards, Chauncy was the most influential clergyman of his time in New England.

Three years before his death, Chauncy published a book that he had actually written several years earlier. It was a book laying out his reasons for believing in the salvation of all mankind. He had withheld its publication because it was clearly at odds with his own Calvinist faith.[130]

In the book, he explained what he saw as the *"glorious benevolent plan of God."*

> "As the First Cause of all things is infinitely benevolent, 'tis not easy to conceive, that he should bring mankind into existence, unless he intended to make them finally happy. And if this was his intention, it cannot well be supposed, as he is infinitely intelligent and wise, that he should be unable to project, or carry into execution, a scheme that would be effectual to secure, sooner or later, the certain accomplishment of it."[131]

Thomas Fessenden

Thomas Fessenden was born in Cambridge, MA in 1739. He graduated from Harvard in 1758 and was a Congregationalist pastor in Walpole, New Hampshire from 1767 until his death in 1813.

> "The advocates for endless sin and misery still continue God's creation and kingdom divided and deranged; God is not and never can be all in all, according to them, to the whole of it . . . Some of them say Christ died only for a few, but all for whom he died will be saved. Others say he died for all, and yet finally will lose most of his redeemed. But neither of them can give a satisfactory reason for the endless duration of sin and misery, nor reconcile it to the

benevolence, holiness, wisdom, and even justice of God."[132]

Benjamin Rush

Benjamin Rush (1745-1813) was a signer of the Declaration of Independence, a delegate to the Continental Congress and a close friend of John Adams and Thomas Jefferson. In fact, it was Rush who reconciled the relationship between those two former presidents – who had been political enemies for years – by encouraging them to resume writing to each other.

Rush was a practicing physician, professor of medicine at the University of Pennsylvania and the founder of Dickinson College. He favored the abolition of slavery and was a pioneer in the study and treatment of mental illness, insisting that the insane had a right to be treated humanely and with dignity. He was also cofounder and vice president of the Philadelphia Bible Society.

Rush was brought up as a Calvinist who focused on God's absolute power to accomplish His will. However, he was uncomfortable with the idea that God chooses to only save some, not all. He then studied Arminian theology which taught that God desires to save all, but that He has given each person sovereignty over his own free will.

Rush concluded that Calvinists were right about God's power, and Arminians were right about His love.

> "The doctrine of universal salvation . . . embraced and reconciled my ancient Calvinistical and my newly adopted Arminian principles. From that time I have never doubted upon the subject of the salvation of all men."[133]

Elhanan Winchester

Elhanan Winchester (1751-1797) was a Baptist preacher

who attracted large crowds with his great memory for Scripture and his enthusiastic speaking style. He, too, began as a strict Calvinist and later became convinced that the Bible taught ultimate restoration.

He founded the Universal Baptist Church in Philadelphia, wrote several books and was a committed abolitionist. Prior to his founding of a church for slaves in South Carolina, no local minister had ever allowed slaves to attend church.[134]

In a series of *Four Dialogues Between a Minister and His Friend*, he speaks of God's amazing grace and supreme power as the basis for his belief in ultimate restoration.

> "Let me ask you seriously, did not Christ make a full and complete offering and propitiation for the sins of the whole world? Is it not certain that his merits were far greater than the demerits of all mankind? Is he not the lamb of God, who taketh away the sin of the world? If Christ died for all men, without exception, as you grant, and removed all their iniquities, and bore them away, and reconciled all to God by his death while they were enemies; much more as he has paid so great a price for their ransom, he will recover them out of their lost estate, and save them by his life.

> "I conclude, that let sin be ever so great, the grace of God is greater . . . Therefore if you magnify sin, and insist upon the greatness of its demerit, I will endeavour to magnify the all powerful Redeemer above it, and speak of his power to redeem all the human race for whom he shed his blood ... Christ being far more infinite to save, than sin can be to destroy; and as he has undertaken to redeem and bring back those who were lost, there is no danger of

his failing to perform it."[135]

Edward Beecher

Edward Beecher was a noted theologian of the 19th century (1803-1895). He was the brother of Harriet Beecher Stowe, who wrote *Uncle Tom's Cabin*. Like his sister, he was a strong opponent of slavery. Beecher served as pastor of Park Street Church in Boston, MA and later as the first president of Illinois College at Jacksonville where he helped organize the first anti-slavery society in Illinois.

When I was in seminary, his book *History of Opinions on the Scriptural Doctrine of Retribution* first introduced me to the concept of ultimate restoration and made a tremendous impact on my life.

Beecher was convinced that what the Bible revealed about the essential goodness of God's nature and character ruled out the common belief in endless punishment.

> "I regard the doctrine of future eternal punishment on the basis of the fall in Adam, as an impossibility with God. What God's nature is, we know. He has so clearly revealed it in Christ that we cannot misunderstand it. We know, too, that it cannot produce effects contrary to itself. And the facts alleged as to eternal punishment, on the basis of the fall in Adam, are contrary to the essential nature and character of God."[136]

J. W. Hanson

John Wesley Hanson (1823-1901) was a writer, pastor and historian who wrote several books defending and promoting universal salvation. He is cited as a primary source in the 1911 edition of the *Encyclopedia Britannica* and *New Schaff-Herzog Encyclopedia of Religious Knowledge* articles on universalism.

In a book that examines each use of the word *hell* in the Bible, he explained that it seemed to him,

"... incredible that a wise and benevolent God should have created or permitted any kind of an endless hell in his universe. Has he done so? ... It is our belief that the Bible hell is not the heathen, nor the 'orthodox' hell, but is one that is doomed to pass away when its purpose shall have been accomplished, in the reformation of those for whose welfare a good God ordained it."[137]

The Universalist Church of America

One of the most surprising developments after the Reformation was the establishment of a Protestant denomination in America specifically focused on the issue of universal salvation.

The first general Universalist Convention was held in Oxford, MA in 1785, and the Universalist Church was begun as a denomination in 1793. The denomination prospered during the 18th and 19th centuries, and grew to be the ninth largest Christian denomination in the United States at its peak.[138]

The doctrine of the Universalist Church in its beginning was very similar to other Christian churches. It differed from them primarily in its view that God's goodness would ultimately prevail and provide salvation for all.[139] Many of the leaders and most eloquent proponents within the denomination based their beliefs on what they saw as clear Biblical teaching, as can be seen in an article on the role of the Bible in the Universalist Church written in 1883.

95

"For one hundred years the Universalist denomination in the United States has stood with remarkable unanimity for the Bible as the inspired word of God. Amidst a storm of vituperative charges of infidelity that has burst upon it from the "evangelical" press and pulpit, it has sturdily maintained its loyalty to the Bible, and kept itself practically free from all forms of unbelief. During this period, books defensive of the Scriptures, written by its most eminent clergymen, have neither been few nor insignificant. While vigorously defending its peculiarities of doctrine, it has been a cordon of fire around the arsenal from which it has drawn its munitions of war."[140]

However, as they entered the 20th century, the Universalists, like other mainline Protestant denominations, drifted away from their roots in Scripture and the Christian faith. A decline in membership and financial resources led to its merger with the American Unitarian Association in 1961. The Unitarians were already less Christian and more secular than the Universalists, and after the merger the Unitarians were the dominant branch of the UUA, as can be seen in their stated values and beliefs.[141]

"Unitarian Universalism is a theologically diverse religion in which members support one another in our search for truth and meaning. We have historic roots in the Jewish and Christian traditions, but today individual Unitarian Universalists may identify as Atheist, Agnostic, Buddhist, Humanist, Pagan, or with other philosophical or religious traditions."[142]

The situation today

Not long ago, I asked a random sample of people in front

of the New York City Public Library to take a six question survey about their thoughts on heaven and hell. I wanted to get an idea of what real people really thought about the afterlife, since what people are *supposed* to think and what they *actually* think are often completely different.

I was especially interested in their answers to the last two questions:

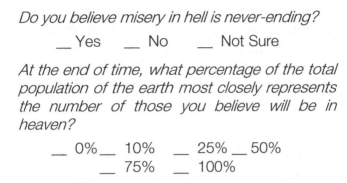

Do you believe misery in hell is never-ending?

__ Yes __ No __ Not Sure

At the end of time, what percentage of the total population of the earth most closely represents the number of those you believe will be in heaven?

__ 0% __ 10% __ 25% __ 50%
__ 75% __ 100%

I was encouraged to find a broad sample of willing participants, male and female of various ages, White, Black, Asian, Latin, Atheist, Buddhist, Christian and Jewish.

Interestingly, about 65% of those taking my survey who professed to be Christians either did *not* believe, or were *not sure* they believed hell was never-ending. And almost 75% of the Christians taking the survey thought that more than half of the total population of the world would eventually be in heaven.

The dominant view held in most of the Christian world today is that hell is a place of conscious torment that never ends, with only a select few escaping its punishment. However, many individual Christians do not actually believe that, and even the official positions within various groups are not as unanimous as some people think.

Eastern Orthodoxy

In the Eastern Orthodox Church of today, the belief in the

ultimate restoration of all is neither heresy nor established belief, but an allowed private theological opinion.

> "The restoration of all . . . a valid possibility according to the Church, although not a doctrine, has a special place in the hopes of saints who pray for the redemption of their enemies, and it expresses our hope for the charity of God. . . . If even one human being is able to forgive and pray for the salvation of the entire cosmos, wouldn't God's providence find a way to allow it to happen?"[143]

Roman Catholicism

There is also a movement in the Roman Catholic Church toward some kind of belief in the salvation of all.

In an article about the Church's teaching on hell throughout the centuries, Avery Cardinal Dulles explained,

> "The fact that something is highly improbable need not prevent us from hoping and praying that it will happen. According to the Catechism of the Catholic Church, 'In hope, the Church prays for "all men to be saved" (1 Timothy 2:4)' (CCC §1821). At another point the Catechism declares: 'The Church prays that no one should be lost' (CCC §1058)."[144]

Swiss theologian Hans Urs von Balthasar is considered one of the most important Catholic intellectuals and writers of the 20th century. He stirred controversy in Europe and in the United States by his teaching that, while one can never be absolutely certain of the final salvation of all, it belongs both to Christian hope and to Christian love that it's possible in the mystery of God's saving grace that all will ultimately be saved.

In the beginning of his book, *Dare We Hope "That All Men*

Be Saved"?, he explained that one cannot divide the divine qualities of justice and mercy in such a way as to leave justice on one side and mercy on the other. Balthasar then told his readers,

> "Now, since precisely this sort of assumption that divine qualities are finite is not acceptable, a dispute arises about whether one who is under judgment, as a Christian, can have hope for all men. I have ventured to answer this affirmatively . . ."[145]

Balthasar died in his home on June 26, 1988, one day before he was to be made a Cardinal by Pope John Paul II.

Popes John Paul II, Benedict XVI and Francis have all supported Balthasar's writings.[146]

Protestantism

As mentioned earlier, the belief in ultimate restoration is not a forbidden doctrine in the Anglican Church. In Congregationalist churches no position is taken on the future of the wicked, but most reject the idea of eternal punishment.[147] In the majority of the Evangelical Protestant churches, however, the belief that hell is eternal conscious torment is clearly the dominant view.[148]

The statement of beliefs of the Southern Baptist Convention, the largest Protestant denomination, states unequivocally that

> "The unrighteous will be consigned to Hell, the place of everlasting punishment."[149]

The Westminster Confession of Faith, the guiding document of the Presbyterian and Reformed Churches, asserts that

> "some men and angels are predestinated unto everlasting life; and others foreordained to

everlasting death."

In Article VII of the same section of the *Confession*, it goes on to say,

> "The rest of mankind God was pleased, according to the unsearchable counsel of His own will, whereby He extends or withholds mercy, as He pleases, for the glory of His sovereign power over His creatures, to pass by; and to ordain them to dishonor and wrath for their sin, to the praise of His glorious justice."[150]

The Statement of Faith of the National Association of Evangelicals affirms their belief in the resurrection of the saved and the lost.

> "We believe in the resurrection of both the saved and the lost; they that are saved unto the resurrection of life and they that are lost unto the resurrection of damnation."[151]

Most evangelical Protestant ministries also clearly state their agreement that suffering in hell never ends. The Statement of Faith of the Billy Graham Evangelistic Association is a clear example.

> "We believe in the resurrection of both the saved and the lost; the saved unto the resurrection of eternal life and the lost unto the resurrection of damnation and eternal punishment."[152]

Most . . . but not all

In recent years, several well-respected scholars have questioned the traditional teaching.[153] Most have concluded that the wicked will ultimately be annihilated,[154] but a number have begun to research and write on the subject from a restoration position.[155]

In his book, *The Inescapable Love of God*, Thomas Talbott, Professor Emeritus of Philosophy, Willamette University, expressed how he came to his conclusions.

> "The Western theological tradition seemed to leave me with a choice between an unjust and unloving God, on the one hand, and a defeated God, on the other. But of course this hardly exhausts the logical possibilities; there remains the additional possibility that it is God's very nature to love, as I John 4:8 and 16 appears to declare, and that he is also wise and resourceful enough to accomplish all of his loving purposes in the end.

> ". . . I now view universal reconciliation as something more than a vague hope of some kind. To the contrary, I now view it as essential to a proper understanding of salvation . . ."[156]

At the second Rethinking Hell Conference held at the prestigious Fuller Theological Seminary in California in June 2015, several speakers and participants alike admitted that they were unaware of the Early Church's teaching on ultimate restoration. A number mentioned they had never heard Biblical support for it. Almost all agreed that the idea was not outside the bounds of faith, and even acknowledged that they were "hopeful" that it was true.[157]

Although holding to the traditional view, one of the primary speakers ended the two-day conference with these words:

> "Universalism is the best story. It's the only one where true, lasting bliss pervades. It's the only one with a perfect ending."[158]

The adventure begins

"Whatcha-doin, Doll?" my wife asked as she saw me

looking intently at my computer screen.

"*Actually, I'm not sure,*" I answered.

"*What do you mean?*"

"*Well, I thought I was just going to update my research paper so I can pass it along to some friends. But I keep discovering new information. It's exciting. But it's starting to look like I'm writing a book.*"

"*Just be careful,*" she said. "*There are a lot of people out there who won't like what you're writing about.*"

"*You really think so?*" I asked.

"*Yes, I do!*"

Chapter 8

What does the Bible really say?
Sheol & Hades

Tears actually began to form in my eyes as my friend left, informing me that he didn't want to have anything to do with me anymore.

We'd known each other for over 12 years. And during that time, we'd had wonderful conversations about life, work and various spiritual topics.

After he moved away, we still kept in touch by email and occasional phone calls. It was always fun talking to him, and I was looking forward to meeting up again at an out-of-town conference where I'd be speaking.

I caught his eye after one of the early sessions, then went over to say hello and tell him how glad I was to see him. He didn't look very happy. He asked if we could talk somewhere alone. We moved to a quiet place in the auditorium. It was not a long conversation.

"George, I think what you are doing is absolutely wrong. You're a false teacher who has now begun to make your errant views public with your blog.

"I want you to know that I contacted the person in charge of this conference to let him know about your unscriptural beliefs. I told him I thought it was totally inappropriate for him to allow you to be a part of this event, and I will continue to follow that practice whenever I hear that you will be speaking somewhere.

"I am not interested in arguing with you about your heretical views."

It's one thing to have people you don't know – and who don't really know you – call you a heretic or a false teacher and tell you to take a hike. It's quite another to have someone you know well do it. Interestingly, my friend's correspondence with the leadership of the conference had no effect because I had already informed them of my views when they first contacted me.

I honestly love my friend. And yes, as far as I'm concerned, he's still my friend. I'm sad he disagrees. But I'm also honestly convinced that I'm not a heretic.

My friend's concern stems from his rightful desire to have his views line up with the true teaching of Scripture. I desire the same thing. The real question that needs to be answered, however, is.

What does the Bible really teach about the ultimate destiny of mankind?

Translations and mistranslations

Translating documents from one language to another isn't as simple as most people think. This is true in part because all words have a history behind how they've been used in the past.

Up until the publication of the novel *1984* by George Orwell, for example, *big brother* was an older sibling who watched out for the other children in the family. Since the book's publication, *Big Brother* has taken on another meaning – a government that spies on its citizens and manipulates them to serve its own needs.

The words have not changed. But the meaning is dramatically different.

In a similar way, the word *hell* has been used so often and for so long to mean unending agony after death, that it conjures up a whole host of images that were never contained in the original English word, and especially not in the underlying Hebrew and Greek words in the Bible.

The term *hell* comes from a word that originally meant *to cover or hide*.[159]

If you lived in England centuries ago and put on a hat to go outside, you'd tell people you were *helling* your head. If your trade was putting slate roofs on houses, you'd be called a *hellier*. *Hell* was the name given to the place under a courtroom where the king's debtors were confined. It was also the place where a tailor flung his leftover scraps of cloth.[160]

The original meaning of the word had nothing to do with after-death punishment.

Translation from one language to another is also difficult because all words have a range of meanings.

For example, the English word *run* can mean an activity that an athlete engages in, a tear in a woman's stocking, something done to a bank when it's in danger of having no money, or scoring a point in a baseball game. The context is often the only thing that will let you know what the word actually means in a sentence. When translating the word *run* into another language, translators need to be very careful that they don't confuse their readers.

In the Bible, four different words are actually translated from Hebrew or Greek to the English word *hell*. They are *Sheol, Hades, Gehenna* and *Tartarus*. As would be expected, they have completely different ranges of meaning in their original languages. *Sheol* and *Hades* refer to *the grave*. *Gehenna* was *a garbage dump* outside Jerusalem. And *Tartarus* was an *underworld place of imprisonment*.

That fact alone should cause us to ask why such different words with very different histories and ranges of meaning are each commonly translated to only one word in English – *hell*.

In this chapter and the chapters that follow, you'll see examples from the Bible that show how these Hebrew and Greek words are used in Scripture. When you see how they're actually used and what they mean in context, *hell* may look a lot different to you.

How is *Sheol* used in the Old Testament?

Sheol is used 65 times in the Old Testament. The King James Version translates it to the word *hell* 31 times, *grave* 31 times and *pit* 3 times.

Sheol is actually a general term meaning *the realm of the dead*.[161] It's used in the Bible to refer to both the righteous and the wicked. The only distinction between the two is that the righteous will not be abandoned in it.[162]

Some of the strongest advocates of endless punishment are quick to say that *Sheol* means what we commonly understand by the word *hell*. William Shedd, considered one of the greatest systematic theologians of the American Presbyterian church, stated categorically that

> ". . . the proof that *Sheol* does not signify Hell would, virtually, be the proof that the doctrine of Hell is not contained in the Old Testament; and

this would imperil the doctrine of the final judgment."[163]

But the term itself does not mean never-ending punishment after death, nor does that meaning come out as a result of how it's used.

For example, when Jacob is shown the blood-stained coat of many colors that he had given to his son Joseph, he says

". . . in mourning will I go down to the grave (*sheol*) to my son."[164]

When Hannah thanks God for answering her prayer, she says,

"The Lord brings death and makes alive; he brings down to the grave (*sheol*) and raises up."[165]

Proverbs 30:15-16 reads,

"There are three things that are never satisfied, four that never say, 'Enough!': the grave (*sheol*), the barren womb, land, which is never satisfied with water, and fire, which never says, 'Enough!'"

In the book of Numbers, not only people, but houses and household goods are said to go down into *Sheol*.

"Korah's men and all their possessions . . . went down alive into the grave (*sheol*), with everything they owned . . . "[166]

In each of the above passages, *Sheol* simply means *grave*, and that's how it's almost always translated. However, in 31 separate instances, the King James Bible translates it to the word *hell*. But even in those instances, the context shows clearly that it's *not* referring to a condition of endless suffering after death. It's referring to either literal death or some type of earthly calamity.

For example, Proverbs 5:5 says of the adulteress,

> "Her feet go down to death; her steps take hold on hell (*sheol*)."

Where do the feet of the adulteress go? The first part of the sentence actually tells us. They go down to death. So the New International Version translates the passage,

> "Her feet go down to death; her steps lead straight to the grave."

When Jonah was swallowed by the great fish, the King James Version says he is in *hell*.

> ". . . out of the belly of hell (*sheol*) cried I, and thou heardest my voice."[167]

None of the modern versions translate it that way. They recognize that Jonah was referring to the place of his ensuing death and translate it accordingly.

> "From the depths of the grave I called for help, and you listened to my cry."

In a similar manner, David says he expects to be delivered from *hell* in Psalm 16:10.

> "For thou wilt not leave my soul in hell (*sheol*); neither wilt thou suffer thine Holy One to see corruption."

The context shows that David is referring to where his body would decay. Thus, the modern translation,

> "you will not abandon me to the grave, nor will you let your Holy One see decay."

Interestingly, except for the King James Version and its revision, the New King James Version, none of the major modern translations of the Bible use the word *hell* in the

Old Testament at all.

That includes the American Standard Version, the New American Standard Version, the Revised Standard Version, the New Revised Standard Version, the English Standard Version, the New International Version, the Revised English Bible, the Amplified Bible, the New American Bible, the New Living Translation, the Contemporary English Version, and the New Century Version.

How is *Hades* used in the New Testament?

The Greek word *Hades* is used 10 or 11 times in the New Testament, depending on the underlying text.[168]

The King James translates it as *hell* all 10 times. The original NIV only translates it that way in the parable of the Rich Man and Lazarus.[169] And none of the other major translations ever translate it as *hell*. Like *Sheol* in the Old Testament, *Hades* refers to the *grave* or *death*, or figuratively to destruction, downfall, calamity or punishment in this world.

Looking at how *Hades* is actually used in context in the New Testament makes it clear that it's not referring to a place of endless, conscious torment after death.

For example, *Hades* is translated as *depths* in connection with the judgment pronounced on the city of Capernaum,

> "And you, Capernaum, will you be lifted up to the skies? No, you will go down to the depths (*hades*)."[170]

Cities clearly do not go to places of torment after death. They are overthrown and destroyed, with their reputations discredited.

In some of the New Testament passages, the Greek word is left untranslated in the modern versions. For example, in

Matthew 16:18, Jesus refers to the gates of *Hades* when He says,

> ". . . on this rock I will build my church, and the gates of *Hades* will not overcome it."

Gates are defensive structures. The imagery that Jesus uses is of a Church on the offense, attacking the gates of *Hades*. Rather than teaching the endless punishment of those locked up in hell, Jesus is saying that His Church will attack and destroy the enemy's gates, bringing release to those held captive by it.

Similarly, Jesus tells the apostle John that He holds the *"keys of death and Hades."*[171] Jesus is certainly not the devil's doorkeeper. He does not lock the door to keep the captives inside. The gates of death and *Hades* open to Him. He is the Victor who defeats His enemies and releases the captives.[172]

There is actually a place in the New Testament that specifically says *Hades* must *give up* its dead! So it cannot refer to a place of unending torment. It's only temporary.[173]

> "The sea gave up the dead that were in it, and death and *Hades* gave up the dead that were in them . . ."[174]

The Rich Man and Lazarus

There is one place where the original NIV translators kept *hell* as the word for *Hades* in the New Testament. It's the well-known parable that Jesus told of the Rich Man and Lazarus.[175] In my experience, this has been the passage most often brought up to support the idea that the Bible clearly teaches endless punishment. But does it?

> "The time came when the beggar died and the angels carried him to Abraham's side. The rich man also died and was buried. In hell, where

he was in torment, he looked up and saw Abraham far away, with Lazarus by his side. So he called to him, 'Father Abraham, have pity on me and send Lazarus to dip the tip of his finger in water and cool my tongue, because I am in agony in this fire.'

"But Abraham replied, 'Son, remember that in your lifetime you received your good things, while Lazarus received bad things, but now he is comforted here and you are in agony. And besides all this, between us and you a great chasm has been fixed, so that those who want to go from here to you cannot, nor can anyone cross over from there to us.'

"He answered, 'Then I beg you, father, send Lazarus to my father's house, for I have five brothers. Let him warn them, so that they will not also come to this place of torment.'

"Abraham replied, 'They have Moses and the Prophets; let them listen to them.'

"'No, father Abraham,' he said, 'but if someone from the dead goes to them, they will repent.'

"He said to him, 'If they do not listen to Moses and the Prophets, they will not be convinced even if someone rises from the dead.'"

At first glance, it certainly looks like there's no way around understanding this parable as promoting the idea of endless, conscious torment. After all, the rich man is in *hell*. He is *"in torment and agony in this fire."* A great chasm has been fixed between the rich man and Lazarus. And those who want to cross over that chasm cannot.

However, if we take a closer look at the passage, a few things bring that interpretation into question.

First of all, the rich man was not in *hell*.

As mentioned earlier, the English word *hell* automatically brings to mind never-ending punishment. But as we have just seen, the Greek word Jesus actually used here does not communicate that idea at all.

Jesus said the rich man was in *Hades,* and Scripture specifically says that *Hades,* as a place of punishment, does not last forever. *Hades* will one day give up the dead who are in it and will itself be cast into the lake of fire.

The next thing we should note is that this is a parable.[176] Jesus is telling a fictional story to teach certain truths to His listeners.[177]

The audience for this parable was made up of two distinct groups of people. One group, the tax collectors and sinners, were spiritually poor and recognized their need for God. The other group, made up of the Pharisees and teachers of the law, were materially rich and had deceived themselves into thinking they were favored by God. Like the rich man in the parable, many of those religious leaders were actually clothed in purple and fine linen and lived in luxury every day.

In this parable, Jesus alluded to an Egyptian folktale that both the religious leaders and the tax collectors were familiar with.[178] But He told it with a very important twist.

The story known to His listeners was about a poor scholar and a rich tax collector. After the two men died, one of the poor scholar's colleagues had a dream. In his dream, he saw the fate of the two men in the next world. The poor scholar was in *"gardens of paradisal beauty, watered by flowing streams."* But the rich tax collector was standing on the bank of a stream, trying to reach the water but unable to do so.

In the original folktale, the Pharisees and teachers of the law would have identified with the poor scholar since they were also scholars who prided themselves on their knowledge of Moses and the prophets. They looked with marked disdain on the tax collector who they considered a great sinner simply by virtue of his occupation. In an absolutely brilliant move, Jesus turned the tables on his listeners and identified the religious leaders *not* with the hero in the story, but with the villain. They were the ones who were rich in this world's goods, but poor in the eyes of God.

Jesus wasn't relating definitive facts about the afterlife. He was using the story to communicate specific truth about this life. The pride and hypocrisy of the religious leaders kept them from understanding what Moses and the prophets taught.[179]

The last thing to note about this passage is that the parable was told *before* Jesus had risen from the dead.

A great chasm separated the rich man from Lazarus. But there is nothing in the account that says that the chasm will always be there. Neither Abraham, nor the rich man, nor Lazarus could do anything to make it possible to go from one side of the chasm to the other. That was the purpose of Jesus' death and resurrection. God bridged the chasm through Him.[180]

Consequences

Beliefs have consequences. Sometimes the consequences bring sadness. I was sad to watch my friend walk away.

But the beliefs I shared with him, and those expressed in this book, are not new.

Most of what I've written has been an attempt to inform people today of beliefs that were held by the Christian Church in the earliest years of its existence when it was closest to the Apostles and its influence on the surrounding culture was the greatest.

I miss my friend, and hope that someday our friendship will be restored. Who knows? Maybe he'll read my book and change his mind.

After all, this is a book about restoration.

Chapter 9

What does the Bible really say?
Gehenna & Tartarus

Not all my friends think I'm a false teacher or a heretic when they learn that I believe God will ultimately restore all His creation. In fact, most are rather intrigued.

That was the case with Don. We were having lunch at a restaurant on New York's West Side, and our conversation went something like this.

"To tell you the truth, George, I've never heard anyone try to argue that position from Scripture," he said. *"I honestly wish it were true. I wish I could believe that God will somehow save everyone. But I have to go on what the Bible actually teaches. And it's pretty clear from Scripture that you're wrong."*

"Am I?" I asked.

"Of course you are," he responded. *"Jesus Himself*

talked more about hell than any other New Testament writer. I'd love to think you're right. But if I have to choose between you and Jesus, there's no question who wins. And it's not you!"

"Fair enough," I agreed. *"If it were between me and Jesus, He definitely wins.*

However, what if Jesus is actually on my side? What if His references to what we call hell had nothing to do with never-ending torment? What if that idea never crossed the minds of the people who were listening to Him when He spoke?"

"It'll be a hard sell," Don said. *"But I'm willing to listen. To tell you the truth, I actually hope you're right!"*

Jesus on hell

Like my friend, people have often said that Jesus spoke of hell more often than any of the other New Testament writers. That claim is actually true. But it's also *not* true at the same time.

The claim is based on the number of times Jesus used the Greek word *Gehenna,* the term most commonly translated as *hell* in modern versions of the Bible. *Gehenna* is used 12 times in the New Testament, and 11 of those times it's used by Jesus Himself. The other use is in the book of James.[181]

So if we're looking at how many times Jesus used the word that's translated *hell* in English, compared to how many times others in the New Testament used that same word, we'd be correct in saying that Jesus spoke of *hell* more often than anyone else.

However, the real issue is not how many times Jesus used a particular word. The real issue is what Jesus meant when He used it . . . and what His listeners understood when they heard it.

One of the most surprising discoveries for me when I looked into what *Gehenna* actually referred to and how the word was used, was that it had nothing to do with endless torment after death.

It didn't mean that in the Old Testament. It didn't mean that during the time of Jesus. It didn't mean that in literature outside the Bible. And it didn't mean that for Jesus and James in the New Testament.

What was Gehenna?

Gehenna is derived from Hebrew words referring to a valley, the Valley of Hinnom.[182] That valley is mentioned a total of 13 times in the Old Testament, always as a literal valley located outside the ancient city of Jerusalem.[183]

The first time it takes on a negative meaning is when we're told that it was the place where two Old Testament kings burned their children alive as part of their idolatrous worship rituals.

According to the ancient rabbis, this was a truly horrific practice. The head of the idol was like that of an ox, with the rest of the body resembling a man. It was hollow, and a fire was kindled inside. The children being sacrificed were then laid in the arms of the idol. The particular part of the valley where the sacrifices were made was called *Topheth*, which means either *a drum*, because the cries of the children sacrificed there were drowned out by that instrument, or *to burn*, because that was where the children were sacrificed to the flames.[184]

This horrendous practice was condemned everywhere in the Scriptures. When King Josiah instituted reforms in Judah,

> "He desecrated Topheth, which was in the Valley of Ben Hinnom, so no one could use it to sacrifice his son or daughter in the fire to Molech."[185]

The valley later became the common dump for all the refuse of the city, including the dead bodies of animals, criminals and all kinds of waste. Fires were kept burning to destroy the odor and germs that were prevalent, and the fire, smoke and worms that resulted made it a horrible place in the eyes of the Jews.

The Old Testament prophet Jeremiah predicted that the valley would become a place of intense judgment in the future because of the horrendous evil the people committed.[186]

But the judgment he referred to was on earth.

It was a prediction of the future destruction of Jerusalem after a long and bitter siege. The bodies of the dead would be given as food to the birds of the air and the beasts of the earth. The city would become an object of scorn. And all who passed by would be appalled. That sentence was literally carried out when the city was destroyed in 587/86 BC. After the judgment, the city was later rebuilt and restored.

Gehenna in the time of Jesus

What comes to your mind when you hear the word *Auschwitz?*

In the future, it's possible that the word will take on a more metaphorical meaning. But right now, while the actual place still exists as a museum and in the memories of some who knew it firsthand, it reminds us of the repulsion, shame and horrible deaths experienced by those who suffered in Nazi concentration camps in World War II.

During the time of Jesus, *Gehenna* was well-known as a specific location near Jerusalem that had been associated with gross idolatry in the past and was then used as the common sewer of the city.

The corpses of the worst criminals were flung into it

unburied, and fires were lit to purify the contaminated air. For the Jews of that day, it also implied the severest judgment that a Jewish court could pass on a criminal – throwing his unburied body into the fires and worms of that polluted valley.[187]

Like Auschwitz, *Gehenna* was a place the people of Jesus' day could actually visit. It spoke to them of repulsion, shame and horrible death. Instead of experiencing honor like their ancestors whose bodies were treated reverently when they died, those cast into *Gehenna* would experience the immense dishonor associated with those whose bodies had been disposed of in a dump to become an object of scorn for the masses.

Solomon expressed very well the thought that would be in the minds of the 1st century Jewish leaders who listened to Jesus.

> "A man may have a hundred children and live many years; yet no matter how long he lives, if he cannot enjoy his prosperity and does not receive proper burial, I say that a stillborn child is better off than he."[188]

Gehenna was definitely a reference to God's judgment. But it was a judgment on earth. It was considered a temporary place of punishment.[189] It never meant endless punishment beyond the grave.

Its use outside Scripture

The authors of the Apocrypha written between 500-150 BC, Philo who wrote around AD 40, and Josephus who wrote from AD 70-100, all refer to the future punishment of the wicked, but none of them ever use the word *Gehenna* to describe it.

It wasn't until after the destruction of Jerusalem that the term began to take on a meaning associated with after-death punishment.[190] And even then, it didn't refer to a place of *endless* punishment.

Origen studied Hebrew for the express purpose of interpreting Scripture. He tells us that his studies revealed what the Jews really meant by *Gehenna*. Besides its primary meaning of the Valley of Hinnom outside Jerusalem, it had come to acquire the secondary meaning of punishment with the intent to purify.

> ". . . seeking to ascertain what might be the inference from the heavenly Jerusalem belonging to the lot of Benjamin and the valley of Ennom, we find a certain confirmation of what is said regarding the place of punishment, intended for the purification of such souls as are to be purified by torments, agreeably to the saying: 'The Lord cometh like a refiner's fire, and like fullers' soap: and He shall sit as a refiner and purifier of silver and of gold.'"[191]

The first Jewish reference to *Gehenna* as a place of future punishment dates from the 2nd century AD.[192] It's part of a commentary on a passage in the book of Isaiah where the author explains that the wicked shall be judged in *Gehenna* until the righteous say concerning them, "*We have seen enough.*"[193]

After studying the writings of the ancient rabbis, contemporary Jewish scholar and rabbi Simcha Paull Raphael explained their understanding of *Gehenna*.

> "The generally accepted belief was that the punitive tortures of *Gehenna* are time-limited, not eternal . . . *Gehenna* was conceived of as a temporary abode widely believed to last a maximum of twelve months . . . The Rabbis always maintained that in addition to its punitive aspects, *Gehenna* served as a realm of

purgation and purification."[194]

Its use in Scripture

The best way to get a clear understanding of what Jesus and James meant when they used the word *Gehenna* is by looking carefully at what they actually said.

The consequences of sin

The first three uses of the word in the New Testament are by Jesus in the Sermon on the Mount.

The popular religious authorities in Jesus' day were not that different from some of the popular religious leaders today. Much of what they said and taught was clearly right. But in their attempt to guard and clarify what they saw as the *Law of God*, they also added ideas that were not consistent with that Law. They told everyone that what they taught was what God's Word said. In reality, what they taught was too often what they themselves said.

In contrast, Jesus brought attention to the true meaning of the Scriptures that the Jewish leaders had misunderstood and misinterpreted.

The first time Jesus refers to *Gehenna*, He explains what murder is really all about.

> "You have heard that it was said to the people long ago, 'Do not murder, and anyone who murders will be subject to judgment.' But I tell you that anyone who is angry with his brother will be subject to judgment. Again, anyone who says to his brother, '*Raca*,' is answerable to the Sanhedrin. But anyone who says, 'You fool!' will be in danger of the fire of *Gehenna*."[195]

God is concerned with more than outward appearances. For Him, offenses are judged by the motives behind them

121

as well as by the actions themselves. Jesus is here referring to three degrees of legal penalties and how they relate to the motives of the heart.

The first level is anger against a brother without cause. The judgment Jesus refers to is one of the lower courts of the Jews.

The second level of offense is contempt, expressed by the derogatory term *Raca* or *shallow brain*. This is punishable at the level of the Sanhedrin, the highest religious and civil tribunal. They judged the greatest offenders of the law.

The third level is hatred, as expressed by the term *moros* in Greek. That word means

> "morally worthless, a scoundrel, a more serious reproach than '*Raca*,' the latter scorns a man's mind and calls him stupid; *moros* scorns his heart and character . . ."[196]

This level deserves not only death, but also the great shame associated with having one's dead body thrown as garbage on the *Gehenna* fires. Jesus was not talking about endless torment. His purpose here, as at many other times during His ministry, was to show that God is not only interested in outward actions. He's also interested in the inward motives behind those actions.

Just a few verses later, still in the context of how God looks on the heart and not just on actions, Jesus equates lust in the heart with adultery.

> "I tell you that anyone who looks at a woman lustfully has already committed adultery with her in his heart. If your right eye causes you to sin, gouge it out and throw it away. It is better for you to lose one part of your body than for your whole body to be thrown into *Gehenna*. And if your right hand causes you to sin, cut it off and

throw it away. It is better for you to lose one part of your body than for your whole body to go into *Gehenna*."[197]

We hear about adultery, pornography and various forms of sexual immorality so often today as it relates to the lives of celebrities, politicians, sports figures and others, that it's easy to think of it as not a big deal. But if you've ever been hurt by some form of sexual infidelity, or if you know others who have, you can understand the depth of pain that can come from what Jesus is talking about.

Jesus was telling His listeners to deal with lust decisively. It's dangerous and destructive. In fact, it would be better to live without the advantage of a right eye, hand or foot than to experience the moral, psychological, and often physical consequences associated with sexual sin. He likens those consequences to the disgusting, shameful death associated with having one's dishonored and putrid corpse thrown into the *Gehenna* dump.

The focus of Jesus' statements in these verses isn't on the duration of punishment in the afterlife. It's on the importance of pursuing a Godly lifestyle in this life. He's telling His listeners to make whatever sacrifices are necessary here and now to keep away from sin!

The fire of *Gehenna*

In a parallel passage in the book of Mark, Jesus adds a comment about the nature of *Gehenna*. He says it's a place where the

"worm does not die and the fire is not quenched."[198]

Doesn't *unquenchable* fire refer to fire that continues on and on forever, and never goes out?

No.

The real meaning of unquenchable fire is not that it keeps

burning forever. The real meaning is that the fire doesn't go out until it does what it's intended to do. It's not *put out* or *quenched* until its purpose is accomplished.

The historian Eusebius says that certain martyrs of Alexandria were burned in *inextinguishable fire*, even though the fire he was referring to was extinguished in the course of an hour.[199] It was *put out* or *quenched* after it had accomplished its purpose. Josephus said that the fire on the altar of the Jerusalem Temple was *unquenchable and always burning,* although that fire had gone out and the Temple was destroyed at the time of his writing.[200]

Jesus wasn't referring to the duration of punishment in the afterlife in this passage. He was saying that the fire and worm will completely accomplish their purifying purpose of ridding the area of disease and filth. Notice, too, that the comment says nothing about the person or the person's body that is thrown into *Gehenna*. It's the fire that's not quenched, and the worm that doesn't die.

In the same context and between two of the *Gehenna* passages in the Sermon on the Mount, Jesus says,

> "I tell you the truth, you will not get out until you have paid the last penny."[201]

The punishment Jesus is talking about is of limited duration. The offender will not get out *until* the penalty has been paid. Release follows.

Destroying soul and body in *Gehenna*

In two passages, Jesus tells His disciples,

> "Do not be afraid of those who kill the body but cannot kill the soul. Rather, be afraid of the One who can destroy both soul and body in *Gehenna*."[202]

Isn't Jesus warning us to be afraid of God who will

destroy souls and bodies in hell? Again, the answer is actually no.

The Greek word translated as *soul* in these passages is also translated as *mind, life* and *heart* in other passages in the New Testament.[203] Just a few verses later, and in the same set of instructions, Jesus uses this same word to tell His disciples,

> "Whoever finds his *life* will lose it, and whoever loses his *life* for my sake will find it."[204]

There is more to your life than just your physical existence. Your reputation and purpose for living, your desires and emotions, your thoughts and ideas are all part of your life or soul. Those things cannot be taken away by men, even if those men are able to put an end to your physical existence. That has been seen countless times when people have died for an important cause. Their ideas, desires and purposes in life often carry great influence far beyond their deaths.

But God is far greater than any human being. He is able to completely destroy both the soul and the body in the *Gehenna* fires. He can bring a complete end not only to someone's physical life, but also to their reputations, goals, desires and purposes. That, too, has been seen countless times in history when evil men have died and the truth about the kind of people they really were comes to light.

In the context of the passages in both Matthew and Luke, Jesus follows His statements about fearing God by reassuring His disciples that it's not God's purpose to destroy them.

On the contrary, Jesus tells them that God loves them and cares for them.

> "Are not two sparrows sold for a penny? Yet not one of them will fall to the ground apart from the will of your Father. And even the very

hairs of your head are all numbered. So don't be afraid, you are worth more than many sparrows."[205]

A son of *Gehenna*

Gehenna is again used by Jesus in the second of a series of seven woes that He pronounces on the religious leaders because of their hypocrisy.

> "Woe to you, teachers of the law and Pharisees, you hypocrites! You travel over land and sea to win a single convert, and when he becomes one, you make him twice as much a son of *Gehenna* as you are."[206]

In the context of the Jews who were listening to Jesus speak, calling someone a *"son of Gehenna"* simply meant that his heart was corrupt and his character vile. In some ways, it's not that different from people in our day calling someone they disrespect a *"son of a b----."* It's a comment about the person's character. It does not assume that the person is actually the offspring of a female dog.

Nothing in this verse requires or even suggests that *Gehenna* refers to a place of endless torment.

Condemned to *Gehenna*

The last reference by Jesus to *Gehenna* is at the very end of the same series of woes, just before He explains with great sadness of heart that Jerusalem will be completely destroyed and left desolate. He says to the religious leaders,

> "You snakes! You brood of vipers! How will you escape being condemned to *Gehenna*?"[207]

The verse is referring to the literal destruction of Jerusalem that would take place in AD 70. The attacking

Roman legions besieged the city, conquered it and tore down the Temple. 600,000 people, including many of the Jewish religious leaders, were killed and had their bodies burned in the conflagration.

Like the criminals whose bodies they had thrown out and burned in the fires of the *Gehenna* dump, so their own bodies were thrown out and burned when the city was destroyed. Jesus was talking about their ensuing shameful deaths in this world, not about torture in the next.

The tongue set on fire by *Gehenna*

The last use of *Gehenna* in the New Testament is in the book of James.

> "The tongue also is a fire, a world of evil among the parts of the body. It corrupts the whole person, sets the whole course of his life on fire, and is itself set on fire by *Gehenna*."[208]

A tongue set on fire by *Gehenna* is a profane and vulgar tongue. James isn't speaking at all about a post-mortem place of torment. He's referring to a specific location that was well-known to his readers as a place of corruption. James applied it figuratively to a corrupt tongue.

Those who listened to Jesus and James were familiar with the place they spoke of when they used the word *Gehenna*. It brought to mind ideas of corruption, filth and shame, but not anything like the meaning that is pre-packaged in the English word *hell*.

They did not think of it as a place of endless punishment beyond the grave. If it hadn't been translated to such a loaded word in English, we wouldn't either.

Tartaros

The last word translated as *hell* in the New Testament is the Greek word *Tartaros*.

"God did not spare angels when they sinned, but cast them into *Tartaros* and committed them to chains of gloomy darkness to be kept until the judgment."[209]

In Greek mythology, *Tartaros* was the deepest abyss of *Hades*.

It was a proverbial place of punishment in the Greco-Roman culture. Interestingly, the form of the word used by Peter is not a noun. It does not indicate a place. If we were to bring it into a modern context, it would be something like *San Quentined* in English. It really means imprisoned.

Peter's comment is a quotation from a non-Biblical book.[210] He uses it in a way similar to someone in our day alluding to a passage from C.S. Lewis' *The Lion, the Witch and the Wardrobe*. If I said, *"Aslan being offered on the Stone Table is like Christ being offered on the cross,"* I wouldn't be implying that Jesus had a mane and walked on all fours, or that the cross He was crucified on was made of stone. I would simply be using a familiar story to make a point.

Even if Peter were quoting the verse because he was trying to teach something about the nature of hell, the most that could be said from his statement is that *Tartaros* is a holding place *until* judgment. The angels referred to are kept in chains of gloomy darkness *"to be kept until the judgment."*

The imprisonment is not endless.

Hope and change

After hearing of my belief in ultimate restoration, a number of my friends have expressed their hope that I'm right. Others have actually changed their views.

One friend wrote, *"I finished reading your manuscript! You've convinced me with this evidence that truly, God is both Good and just and will completely restore creation to what He intended it to be. . . . I'm giving you a cyberspace hug with tears in my eyes. This is monumental for my faith."*

A different friend said, *"For the first time in my life, I'm really excited about heaven and about what God is going to do."*

As for my friend, Don? The jury's still out. Maybe he just needs to talk about it some more.

Chapter 10

How long is *forever* anyway?
Aion, Olam & Kolasis

It started out as a simple conversation between a father and his young daughter.

The family had decided to vacation at the beach. The sun was shining. The sky was clear. The ocean sparkled as it reflected the bright blue sky in a way that made the sea and the sky almost look as one. They were walking along the water's edge picking up shells when the daughter spoke up.

"The water looks like it goes on forever, doesn't it Daddy?

"Yes, it does sweetheart," her father answered.

"But of course it doesn't. Does it?" she responded. *"There's really an end out there somewhere, even if we can't see it. Right?"*

"That's right, darling. The ocean's big. But if you sail on it long enough, you'll find land on the other side."

131

The little girl picked up a shell and threw it into the ocean. *"How long is forever, Daddy . . . really?"* she asked.

That was a question he wasn't expecting. He stopped, looked at her for a moment, then said, *"That's a very big question for a little girl. What made you think about that?"*

She looked up at her dad. Tears were beginning to form in her eyes when she replied. *"Ashley told me that all the people who don't go to her church will go to hell and be there forever! But we'll get out of there someday, won't we, Daddy?"*

Her father smiled, picked her up and gave her a big hug.

"Don't worry, sweetheart," he said. *"Ashley's a good girl and a good friend. But what she told you about hell isn't true. Not all the people who don't go to her church will go there. And I don't think we'll go there either. But for those who do, the Bible says hell is a lot like the ocean. It may go on for a very long time, but eventually it does have an end."*

Punishment that never ends?

Forever is a *very* long time!

Whether it's measured in hours, days or years, or is some kind of constant state of being, the concept of conscious suffering that never ends is a horror beyond our imaginations. I often wonder if people who say they believe in endless punishment have ever really thought about what it actually means.

Not long ago, a friend told me his reason for believing that God punishes forever. *"Because God is holy,"* he said, *"He cannot look on sin. He must punish it."*

But punishment for sin isn't really the issue. We see sin punished all the time in this life.

However, punishment that goes on forever and *never . . . ever . . . ever . . . ever . . . ever . . .* ends is a completely different matter. It brings to mind cruel tyrants who torture subjects who don't do their bidding.

The words translated *forever, eternal* or *everlasting* in our English Bibles are *olam* in Hebrew, and *aion* in Greek. And they actually mean

> "a period of time – longer or shorter, past or future – the boundaries of which are concealed, obscure, unseen or unknown."[211]

They do not mean never-ending. They mean that the end is not known.

Olam and *aion*

Olam and *aion* are relative terms – words where the meaning is determined by the things they relate to.[212] Now that may sound strange at first, but we actually use relative terms all the time. For example, the word *tall* means different things depending on the subject it's modifying. NBA basketball player Dwight Howard is a *tall* man. One World Trade Center is a *tall* building. Denali is a *tall* mountain. But they are not all the same size.

What *tall* is to size, the Hebrew and Greek words generally translated as forever are to duration. That will become very clear when we look at how they're actually used.[213]

Forever in the Old Testament

Forever in the Old Testament regularly refers to things that have or will come to an end.[214]

The book of Exodus explains that a slave who wanted to remain with his master and not go free must be taken before the judges, have his ear pierced, and then he would be his master's slave *forever*.[215] Since neither the slave nor his master knew how long he would live, the length of service couldn't be known. At most, he would serve his master until he died. Several modern versions translate the verse with that understanding in mind, *"he shall serve him for life."*[216]

In many places in the Old Testament, the sacrifices and offerings made by the priests are said to be established by God *forever.*[217]

The sacrificial system lasted for a very long time, almost 1,000 years. But it eventually came to an end. The first Temple was destroyed by the Babylonians in 587/86 BC, and the rebuilt Temple was destroyed by Roman forces in AD 70.

There's no longer a Jewish priesthood. There's no longer a Temple in Jerusalem. There's no longer a system of sacrifices being offered. The purpose for that system was fulfilled, and it was no longer needed. It's now been superseded by the New Covenant in Christ.

The Hebrew word translated as *forever* in these passages did not and could not mean endless. If it did, the Jews would have been perfectly justified in rejecting the Christian religion because it proclaimed the end of statutes and ordinances which they had been told again and again were to be *forever.* If they could have established that meaning for the word, they would have had an unanswerable argument against Christianity![218]

The everlasting hills

In Genesis and Deuteronomy we are told that the hills are *everlasting.*[219]

Mountains and hills last a long time. But they won't last forever. Nor were they intended to. At some unknown time in the future, the mountains and hills that we see every day will no longer be there.

> "For the mountains shall depart, And the hills be removed, But My kindness shall not depart from you . . ."[220]

134

God's disfavor

God told Jonah to go to the wicked city of Nineveh and tell the people there to repent. Instead, Jonah went down to the sea, got into a boat and headed in the opposite direction.

But God didn't take no for an answer!

When He sent a violent storm on the sea, the sailors threw Jonah overboard and he was swallowed by a great fish especially prepared for the occasion. Inside the fish, Jonah had a change of heart and decided to pray. In his prayer he tells how long he expected to be imprisoned.

> "To the roots of the mountains I sank down; the earth beneath barred me in forever.[221]

Jonah didn't know how long his situation would last. In this case, *forever* meant three days and was followed by his release.

Jerusalem and the Temple

God said He would cause His Name to rest on Solomon's temple *forever.*[222] He kept it there until He allowed it to be destroyed by a commander in the army of Babylon who

> "set fire to the temple of the LORD . . . Every important building he burned down."[223]

Isaiah 32:14-17 tells us that God will destroy the fortified city of Jerusalem and leave it desolate *forever* . . . *until* He pours out His Spirit and righteousness prevails.

> "For the palace will be forsaken, the populous city deserted; the hill and the watchtower will become dens forever . . . until the Spirit is poured upon us from on high"[224]

The sun, moon and stars

According to Psalm 148, the sun, moon and stars will last *forever and ever!*[225] But even they will not last for an endless eternity.

> "Then I saw a new heaven and a new earth, for the first heaven and the first earth had passed away . . ."[226]

The eternal God

What about God? Doesn't He exist outside of time? Isn't He the *eternal* God? Doesn't He exist from *everlasting to everlasting*?

Absolutely.

God is truly *eternal.* He did not have a beginning. Nor will He have an end. However, when speaking of God, the term translated *forever* or *everlasting* or *eternal* takes its meaning from Him. The praises in the Psalms tell of His greatness not because the word used necessarily meant eternal or never-ending, but because *He* is the *eternal, never-ending* God.[227]

Forever in the New Testament

In the New Testament, the word *aion* always carries the notion of time, and not eternity.[228]

In fact, it's often translated to the English word *age,* a term more consistent with the idea of an indefinite period of time.

We often use *age* in a way similar to how the New Testament uses *aion.*

We wouldn't be surprised, for example, to hear an evolutionary paleontologist talk of millions of years that comprised the Age of Dinosaurs. Nor would we think it odd to hear a historian refer to the decades that comprised the Victorian Age. If we were caught in a major traffic jam for an hour on the way to work, we might even tell our co-workers that it took an *age* to get through it.

Same word . . . different meanings depending on what it's referring to.

The ages

In the New Testament, *aion* is used to refer to Christ's kingdom when the angel Gabriel tells Mary she will give birth to a son. Describing this Son, the angel says,

> "He will reign over the house of Jacob forever."[229]

Now that certainly seems in English to refer to a kingdom that Jesus will reign over throughout eternity. However, two factors argue against it.

First, the kingdom of Christ will actually come to an end. When Christ has put all His enemies under his feet, including the last enemy which is death, He will hand over the kingdom to God the Father so that God may be all in all.[230] Gabriel's statement to Mary makes clear sense if it is translated literally,

> "And he shall reign over the house of Jacob to the ages."[231]

Second, the Greek word here is used in its plural form. The angel did not say, *to the age.* He said Christ will reign *to the ages.* To translate the phrase *to the forevers* would negate the very concept of an endless period of time.

The plural form of the Greek word *aion* is used several times elsewhere in the New Testament. For example, Paul tells his readers in Corinth about a wisdom of *this* age in contrast to the wisdom of God which He decreed *before* the ages.[232] Later in the same book he talks of those on whom the *end* of the ages has come.[233] In Ephesians he tells us about the ages *to come.*[234] And in his letter to the Colossian Christians, Paul speaks of the mystery that has been kept hidden *"for ages . . . but is now disclosed to the saints."*[235]

It's clear from these passages that there is a present age. There are past ages. And there are future ages. It's also clear that the ages have a beginning and an end. There is a time before the ages, and there is an end of the ages.[236]

Ages may last a long time, but they're not forever.

Endless punishment

In my experience, the passage most often pointed to as the clearest statement in the entire Bible that punishment in hell is endless, is Matthew 25:46.[237] In that verse, Jesus Himself says that the wicked

> "will go away to eternal (aion) punishment, but the righteous to eternal (aion) life."

Remember that *aion,* the Greek word Jesus used here, is the same word we've been talking about. And it's used to refer to both the punishment of the wicked and the life of the righteous.

That verse has been used for over 1,500 years to argue that hell is endless. The reasoning goes like this.

> *Since the Bible clearly teaches that eternal life is endless, it follows that eternal punishment must also be endless. Or put another way, if punishment in this passage is temporary, it would also mean the life that the righteous will experience will also be only temporary.*

That thought was actually introduced in the 5th century by St. Augustine who, as was pointed out earlier, didn't read Greek. It's been considered by many as conclusive proof for that position ever since.

Augustine said,

> "For Christ, in the very same passage, included both punishment and life in one and the same sentence . . . If both are 'eternal,' it follows necessarily that either both are to be taken as long-lasting but finite, or both as endless and perpetual."[238]

One religious writer was so convinced this was true that he stated categorically that anyone who disagreed with him must have been deceived by the devil.

> "The original word is the same in both clauses (aionios); and he must be blinded by Satan in no ordinary degree, who will risk his immortal soul and its eternal interests on interpreting the same word temporary in one clause, and eternal in another, of the same verse; and if the punishment be eternal, there can be no place for annihilation, or for final restitution."[239]

Another boldly asserted that there can be

> "no room for rational doubt here . . . WE MUST EITHER ADMIT THE ENDLESS MISERY OF HELL OR GIVE UP THE ENDLESS HAPPINESS OF HEAVEN."[240]

But is that correct? When the same word is used twice in the same sentence, does it necessarily mean the same thing each time?

Actually, no.

We often use relative terms more than once in the same sentence with a different meaning each time it's used.

For example, if NBA Basketball player Dwight Howard were standing in front of One World Trade Center in New York City, you could honestly say,

"A tall man is standing in front of a tall building."

But no one would think you thought the man and the building were the same size. The word *tall* derives its meaning from what it refers to, in the first instance to a man and in the second to a building.

The same is true for the Greek word *aion* in Matthew 25:46. It should actually be translated,

> "The wicked shall go away into the punishment of the age to come, and the righteous into the life of the age to come."[241]

Jesus is referring to two completely different things – life and punishment. Eternal life is divine life that comes from God. That divine life never ends. Eternal punishment is divine punishment from His hand. The duration of that divine punishment may certainly be temporary, lasting only until it accomplishes its purpose.[242]

There's another passage in the New Testament where this same Greek word is used twice in the same sentence, with the first use clearly referring to what has ended and the second to what never ends. And it's correctly translated in the English versions.

In Romans 16:25-26, the apostle Paul tells us of the

> "mystery hidden for long ages past (aion), but now revealed and made known through the prophetic writings by the command of the eternal (aion) God."

The word translated *long ages past* is the same word in the same sentence as the word translated *eternal*. The first use obviously refers to times that have come to an end, since the mystery that was hidden is now revealed. The second refers to God who is by nature eternal. The meaning in each instance is determined by the subject it's referring to.[243]

The all-important context

If we take the time to look at what Jesus is actually talking about in Matthew 25:46, we'll make an amazing discovery.

Jesus' statement occurs at the end of an extended discourse that He gives privately to His disciples.[244] The question that prompts the entire talk is

". . . what will be the sign of your coming and of the end of the age (aion)?"

Jesus and His disciples begin with an acknowledgment that *ages* have an end. They do not last forever. The Greek word *aion* used here cannot mean endless because Jesus is explaining to His disciples what will happen at the *end* of the *aion.*

Kolasis

So what kind of punishment is Jesus actually referring to in this passage if it's not endless?

The Greek word for *punishment* in Matthew 25:46 is *kolasis.* It was originally used to mean *pruning trees to make them grow better.* In fact, in all Greek literature outside the Bible, it's never used for anything but remedial punishment.[245]

In the ancient world, the idea of punishment by their gods was widespread, with many inscriptions using various forms of the word.[246] These inscriptions make it clear that the punishments they refer to always include the possibility of restoration if a sinner humbly confesses his guilt. The intent is to bring about repentance.

The Greek writer Plato in a dialogue with Socrates makes it very clear that punishment *(kolasis)* must be purposeful.

"If you will think, Socrates, of the nature of punishment, you will see at once that in the

141

opinion of mankind virtue may be acquired; no one punishes the evil-doer under the notion, or for the reason, that he has done wrong, only the unreasonable fury of a beast acts in that manner.

"But he who desires to inflict rational punishment does not retaliate for a past wrong which cannot be undone; he has regard to the future, and is desirous that the man who is punished, and he who sees him punished, may be deterred from doing wrong again.

"He punishes for the sake of prevention ..."[247]

In Scripture, as in the literature of the time, the meaning of the word Jesus used for punishment primarily meant *to curtail, prune, dock . . . then, to check, restrain, punish.*[248] Punishment is designed to cut off what is bad or disorderly.[249]

The word is used only 3 other times in the New Testament.

In Acts 4:21, after Peter and John were questioned by the religious leaders, they were let go.

"They could not decide how to punish (kolasis) them, because all the people were praising God for what had happened."

The desired punishment that the Jewish leaders wanted to inflict clearly had a purpose. They wanted them to change their attitude about Christ.

Peter writes in II Peter 2:9,

"the Lord knows how to rescue the godly from trial, and to keep the unrighteous under punishment until the day of judgment."

The punishment here is clearly not never-ending. Again, there is a definite purpose for it. The unrighteous are to be kept under punishment *until* the day of judgment. When that day comes, they will be released and brought before the Judge.

In I John 4:18, we are told,

> "perfect love drives out fear, because fear has to do with punishment."

Nothing is clearly said in this passage about the nature of the punishment that is referred to except that God's perfect love drives out the fear associated with it.

What kind of punishment does a good God inflict on His creatures? It's the same kind of punishment that Jesus refers to in Matthew 25:46. It's a purposeful punishment designed to restore.

Everlasting destruction

In II Thessalonians 1:9, the apostle Paul tells his readers that those who do not know God and do not obey the gospel of our Lord Jesus will be

> "punished with everlasting destruction and shut out from the presence of the Lord . . ."

Those are pretty strong words! If you were *punished with everlasting destruction* and *shut out from the presence of the Lord*, where else would you be but in hell? Here again, the translation into English is misleading.

As we have seen, the word translated as *everlasting* does not mean never-ending. It means *the end is not known*. The verse definitely talks of punishment, but it does not talk of punishment that never ends.

The actual Greek text of this verse also does not say that those punished will be *shut out* from the presence of the Lord. It simply says that the punishment is *from* the presence of the Lord. Depending on the context, that phrase could mean punishment *away* from or punishment *coming* from the Lord.

A few verses earlier, Paul says that God is just and will punish those who unjustly treated the Thessalonian Christians.[250] He's not talking about punishment that keeps people *shut out* from the presence of the Lord. He's talking about just punishment that comes *from* the presence of the Lord on those who are mistreating His people.

The destruction Paul refers to literally means *ruin or desolation*.[251] In this passage, Paul is simply saying that those who are unjustly persecuting the Thessalonian believers will experience *ruin* from the hand of God in the *age to come*. He's not talking about endless torment. He's talking about how the wicked will be humbled before God, and the plans of their hearts will be brought to nothing, as God justly pays them back for the trouble they have caused His people.

Eternal life

With what I've said so far, do we now have a bigger problem on our hands? What about *eternal life* for the believer? If the word eternal doesn't mean forever, does that mean heaven isn't forever?

Actually no.

The Greek New Testament makes it very clear that those who are in Christ will live in heaven forever. But it doesn't teach that truth with the word translated as *forever*.

For example, when a group of religious leaders tried to trap Him, Jesus explained very clearly that the children of the resurrection are God's children who will *never die*.[252]

Similarly, when Jesus tells His followers that He is the Good Shepherd, He assures them that His sheep hear His voice and will *never perish*.

"My sheep listen to my voice; I know them and

they follow me. I give them eternal life, and they shall never perish; no one can snatch them out of my hand. My Father, who has given them to me, is greater than all; no one can snatch them out of my Father's hand."[253]

When standing in front of Lazarus' tomb, Jesus comforted the dead man's sister, Martha, by telling her that those who believe in Him will *never die*.[254]

In a truly powerful statement in the book of Romans, Paul explains that we are more than conquerors in Christ. In fact, there is nothing that can separate us from the love of God!

". . . neither death nor life, neither angels nor demons, neither the present nor the future, nor any powers, neither height nor depth, nor anything else in all creation, will be able to separate us from the love of God that is in Christ Jesus our Lord."[255]

In I Corinthians 15:42, he tells his readers that the resurrection body is *imperishable*.[256] He explains a few verses later that the mortal will be clothed with *immortality*.[257] For Paul, all of this is based on the guaranteed fact that Christ has been raised from the dead, and in Him all will be *made alive*.[258]

Peter also talks of an incorruptible life kept in heaven for us that can *never perish, spoil or fade*.[259] He goes on to tell us that when the Chief Shepherd appears, we will receive a crown of glory that will *never fade away!*[260]

Do those who put their faith in the finished work of Christ have what we call *eternal life?* The answer is yes. But it's clear from passages that do not use the word *forever.*

More than just time

We tend to think of eternal life as simply being endless

because that's what the words mean to us in our language today. But that's not what they really mean in the Bible. The true focus of the eternal life we have in Christ is much broader and grander than just a long period of time.

The phrase *zoe aionios* that is generally translated *eternal life* or *everlasting life* in our English Bibles occurs 42 times in the New Testament. It primarily means *a life which belongs to God.*[261] It's a different quality of life from our old existence which is characterized by hate, lack of love, sin, pain and death. It's living with the supernatural life of God in us.

Contrary to what many people think, eternal life does not begin in the future.

It's not something that only relates to the ages to come. It's already the possession of those who have entered into a relationship with Christ. Jesus said,

> "whoever hears my word and believes him who sent me has eternal life."[262]

In John 3:36, we read,

> "Whoever believes in the Son has eternal life."

Again in John 6:47,

> "I tell you the truth, he who believes has everlasting life."

And in John 6:54,

> "Whoever eats my flesh and drinks my blood has eternal life."

Jesus said the Father's command *is* eternal life in John 12:50.

> "And I know that his commandment is life everlasting."[263]

God is not limited by time. He is the God who works

out His plan through the *ages* of time. Biblical scholar Marvin Vincent writes,

> "God transcends time; works on different principles and on a vaster scale than the wisdom of time provides; oversteps the conditions and the motives of time; marshals the successive [ages] from a point outside of time, on lines which run out into his own measureless cycles, and for sublime moral ends which the creature of threescore and ten years cannot grasp and does not even suspect."[264]

Eternal life is not only something we *will* have. Eternal life is something we *now* have!

The heavens . . . and heaven

"Daddy?"

"Yes, darling."

"What about the sky? Does that go on forever?"

"Nobody really knows, sweetheart. But I'll tell you what . . . when we get to heaven, let's ask God."

Chapter 11

What are God's judgments all about?

"There's always hope!" Emily said warmly.

Is there? It wasn't that she didn't believe it, or that her friend wasn't sincerely motivated by a desire to be helpful. It's just that *those* words at *that* time sounded a little hollow. All she really wanted was a hug.

Details of the car accident were sketchy. They said alcohol had been served at the party, but there was no evidence that Danny had been driving while intoxicated. He wasn't really a bad kid. He did some things he shouldn't have, of course. All kids did. He just needed more time to grow up. He needed more time to find out what was really important in life. After all, hadn't that been true for her? She came to faith after making a lot of mistakes. Lots of people she knew had the same experience.

Emily had tried to be encouraging. *"There's always hope,"* she whispered. *"It's said that people's whole lives flash before their minds in the last seconds. Maybe Danny made peace with God at the last moment."*

Maybe. But somehow the words didn't really sound hopeful. She loved her son. Nothing would ever change that. Not even death. God was forgiving. She knew that for sure. Danny just needed more time. But there was no more time left.

"Thank you," she told her friend after giving her a hug. *"I certainly need hope."*

When the pastor walked in, everyone sat down quietly. He moved slowly around the closed casket on his way to the podium at the front of the room. He was new at the church, but he seemed like a good person when she spoke to him before the funeral.

"Please, Lord. Give him something hopeful to say," she prayed. But what could he say? Her son was dead. The time he needed was no longer there. Wasn't the Bible clear that after death comes the judgment?

"This is truly a sad day," the pastor began. *"Death is always an unwelcomed guest, but even more so when it comes to someone so young. I spoke to Danny's mother earlier this morning, and she mentioned her love for her son along with his need for 'a little more time.' Let me begin with some words of encouragement for her and for all of us. This comes from the book of James in the Bible – 'Mercy triumphs over judgment!'"*[265]

What did he say? *"Mercy triumphs over judgment?"* Is that true? Does the Bible really say that? Is it possible that God's love and mercy continue after death? If it does, there might still be hope. A hope she could actually hold onto.

Is God conflicted?

In a remarkable conversation between God and Abraham

over the fate of the city of Sodom, Abraham asks a very bold question,

"Will not the Judge of all the earth do right?"[266]

The answer to that question is yes.

God *is* the Judge of all the earth. And He alone *always* does what is right. But what are His judgments all about?

I've had many conversations over the years with people who've told me, *"God is not only loving, He's also just!"*

In fact, it's been stated with such confidence that you'd think this one statement suddenly provided the final answer to all the questions, objections and ethical dilemmas that endless suffering in hell raises. But it actually introduces new questions that bring with them a much greater problem.

Is God internally conflicted?

Is there a hierarchy within God's nature that makes one of His qualities – love – grudgingly submit to another of His qualities – justice?

Is one of God's divine attributes at war with another?

The answer to those questions is no.

God is not conflicted internally. The loving and just elements of His character are not at war with each other. His love is not in opposition to His justice. It was His justice, working together with His love that led to Christ dying on the cross for our sins.

God's judgments are just

Believing that God will one day reconcile to Himself all of His creation does not undermine the fact that God is just.

Justice demands that the punishment inflicted fit the crime committed.[267]

Requiring a life for an eye or a hand for stealing a loaf of bread, for example, is not *just*. It's not *just* to require endless years of pain and suffering for each thought, word or act of sin committed during a person's short life of seventy or eighty years on this earth. And it's also not *just* to require an infinite penalty because the sins are committed against an infinite God.

God is not like earthly despots who torture those who treat them with disrespect. When Jesus was being crucified unjustly, He didn't pour down curses on those who were nailing Him to the cross. He asked His Father to forgive them![268]

God Himself has actually made clear what He considers the just penalty required for sin committed directly against Him.

> "If anyone curses his God, he will be held responsible; anyone who blasphemes the name of the LORD must be put to death."[269]

Notice the penalty. The man is not to be put to death and then tormented forever. He's to be put to death.

If God had left it at that, annihilation would have been the just penalty for sins committed against a holy God. The person who sins dies. But God didn't leave it at that! Because of His love, God did something that was absolutely unexpected. He did something that was remarkable!

God entered the world and personally paid the penalty for sin. And He didn't just pay part of the penalty. He paid the penalty in full. Nothing additional is needed.[270] Sin had to be judged, and the penalty had to be administered. But that's exactly what happened when Christ died on the cross.

God judged sin.

I find it quite interesting that many of those who are most vocal about endless punishment have no difficulty believing that God can forgive the worst sins right up to the point of someone's physical death. They simply don't believe that God's love and forgiveness continue into the ages to come. Instead, they believe God places a limit on His grace. But God's grace is far greater than mankind's sin. In fact, the Apostle Paul tells us,

> ". . . where sin increased, grace increased all the more."[271]

God's judgments are just. But His justice and love do not war against each other. With God, justice and love work together to accomplish His purposes.

God's judgments are purposeful

God didn't create the heavens and the earth and suddenly get surprised by sin. He knew that mankind would sin in all kinds of ways, so He included that in His ultimate plan. And His plans and purposes will not be thwarted.

Since God doesn't change but is the same yesterday, today and forever, the best way to get an understanding of His purposes for judgment *after* death is by looking at His purposes for judgment *before* death.

Limit sin and suffering

Sin is ultimately destructive. It hurts those who commit it, and it also hurts others. It brings pain and suffering to people in the present, and it increases pain and suffering for people in the future.

Infants born to alcoholic parents sometimes enter the world with Fetal Alcohol Syndrome which will affect them throughout their entire lives. Children brought up in abusive homes sometimes carry the negative effects of their learned behavior to the families they later raise.

God allowed pain and suffering to become part of His

creation, but He also placed a limit on how much pain and suffering He will allow.

Our bodies, for example, are designed in such a way that there is actually an upper limit for pain. When that level is reached, the body naturally shuts down. Either the specific area of pain goes numb or the entire body goes unconscious.

God has also placed a limit on the level of pain and suffering that He will allow any one culture to experience or inflict. The clear lessons from Scripture and history are that torturous regimes always come to an end. And morally corrupt cultures either disintegrate or are destroyed.

The Flood of Noah's day came as God's judgment on an earth that was filled with wickedness. The cities of Sodom and Gomorrah were destroyed because not even 10 righteous people could be found in them.

God doesn't hate sinners. He hates sin. His purpose for judgment on the world of Noah and on Sodom and Gomorrah was to put an end to the gross sin existing in those cultures and the impact it would have on other cultures and other generations. The level of sin had gone far enough, and God ended it.

God even has a gracious purpose for physical death. It's not only a way out of suffering. It's ultimately a way out of being bound forever in a sinful state where we must experience the negative effects of our own sin and the sins of others.

Reveal who God is

Another of God's primary purposes for judgment before death is to reveal to the world who He is.

One of the most commonly used phrases in the entire Bible relating to God's judgment is so people will

"know that I am the LORD."

That exact phrase is used over 65 times with the same idea conveyed in different words in many other places. God doesn't punish people for the sake of punishing them. He brings judgment so they will learn that the false deities they worship are impotent. They have no real power. Only the one true God is able to save and deliver.

God brought judgment on Egypt so that His people would know who He is.[272] His action also impacted the Egyptians so that they would know who He is.[273] When Israel turned away from Him to worship idols, God told Ezekiel why He would bring judgment on them.

"Then they will know that I am the LORD."[274]

God also explained to Ezekiel what His purposes were for restoring them. Not only would His *judgments* reveal to them who He is, so would His *grace.*

"I will accept you as fragrant incense when I bring you out from the nations and gather you from the countries where you have been scattered . . . You will know that I am the LORD, when I deal with you for my name's sake and not according to your evil ways and your corrupt practices."[275]

Lead to repentance

Perhaps the most often cited reason for why God brings judgment is so people will see their need for Him and turn away from doing what is wrong. God takes no pleasure in the death of the wicked. His desire is that they turn from their evil ways and live![276]

Psalm 107 tells why those who suffered because they rebelled against God and despised His counsel should be thankful.

"Some sat in darkness and the deepest gloom, prisoners suffering in iron chains, for they had rebelled against the words of God and despised the counsel of the Most High. So he subjected them to bitter labor; they stumbled, and there was no one to help.

Then they cried to the LORD in their trouble and he saved them from their distress. He brought them out of darkness and the deepest gloom and broke away their chains."[277]

The last verse of that Psalm doesn't admonish the reader to consider the great power of God or the justice of His actions. It's a call to the reader to consider the great *love* of the LORD.

"Let those who are wise give heed to these things, and consider the steadfast love of the LORD."[278]

The author of Psalm 119 tells us why the judgments that he experienced from God were good for him. Through the afflictions that resulted from those judgments, he was brought back into fellowship with God.

"Before I was afflicted I went astray, but now I obey your word . . . It was good for me to be afflicted so that I might learn your decrees."[279]

Solomon exhorted his son to submit to God's discipline because His purposes for judgment are good.

"My son, do not despise the LORD's discipline and do not resent his rebuke, because the LORD disciplines those he loves, as a father the son he delights in."[280]

After telling his people that God's judgments on Jerusalem and Judah would result in their destruction and captivity, Isaiah told them why. The judgments would cleanse the city from its sin.[281] The city was later rebuilt and restored.

The prophet Jeremiah told the people that God would make Jerusalem a heap of ruins. He would lay waste the towns of Judah so no one could live there. But why would He do it? He would bring judgment in order to refine and test them.[282] Later, the prophet explained the result of God's refining judgment. Israel would repent and return to their Lord in humility.[283]

God's good purposes for judgment are expressed clearly in the book of Lamentations.

> "For men are not cast off by the Lord forever. Though he brings grief, he will show compassion, so great is his unfailing love. For he does not willingly bring affliction or grief to the children of men."[284]

Through the prophet Zephaniah, God declared that He will bring severe judgment on all the nations. But the judgment is for a purpose – to purify the people so that they will all ultimately call on the name of the LORD and serve Him.[285]

When the prophet Malachi told of the future coming of the Lord to His temple, he explained that He would come as a fire. But He would come as a *refiner's* fire to purify.[286]

The apostle Paul instructed his readers in Corinth to punish one of their members who was involved in gross immorality that he said was of a kind that does not occur even among pagans.[287] What kind of punishment did he call for? Remedial punishment that would ultimately result in salvation.

> ". . . you are to deliver this man to Satan for the destruction of the flesh, so that his spirit may be saved in the day of the Lord."[288]

The issue before us is not the fact of judgment after death. The Bible clearly teaches that man is destined to die, and after that to face judgment.[289] The real issue is whether or not God has a benevolent purpose for His judgments. God is the Redeemer of mankind! And Scripture makes it clear that His purposes for judgment, as His purposes for everything, are redemptive.

> "This is good, and pleases God our Savior, who wants all men to be saved and to come to a knowledge of the truth. For there is one God and one mediator between God and men, the man Christ Jesus, who gave himself as a ransom for all men – the testimony given in its proper time."[290]

God's judgments are in keeping with His nature

God's judgments are just. They're purposeful. And they're also in keeping with His sovereign and gracious nature.

Volumes have been written through the centuries about who God is and what He is like. The qualities talked about are divided up and stated in different ways by different people, but all mention two that are dominant. Interestingly, these two attributes of God relate directly to the questions of salvation and after-death judgment.

When King David thought about where he should put his trust, he pointed to the two aspects of God's nature that are at the heart of who He really is.

> "One thing God has spoken, two things have I heard: that you, O God, are strong, and that you, O Lord, are loving."[291]

Of all the qualities that characterize the God of heaven, His unlimited power and His unfailing love are most important.

God alone has the absolute right and power to do

whatever He wants.

> "In the beginning God created the heavens and the earth."[292]

> "The Most High God rules over the kingdoms of men and sets over them anyone He wishes."[293]

> "The king's heart is in the hand of the Lord; He directs it like a watercourse wherever He wishes."[294]

> "There is no wisdom, no insight, no plan that can succeed against the LORD."[295]

> "The LORD does whatever pleases him, in the heavens and on the earth, in the seas and all their depths."[296]

> "Who works out everything in conformity with the purpose of His will."[297]

> "I know you can do all things; no plan of yours can be thwarted."[298]

> "For nothing is impossible with God."[299]

> "I am the LORD, the God of all mankind. Is anything too hard for me?"[300]

There are no limits on God except those that He Himself has imposed because of the goodness of His nature. God *cannot* do certain things because He *wills not* to do them. Which brings us to the second attribute of God.

Not only is God powerful, He's also loving. In fact, Scripture says He is not simply loving, He *is* love![301]

> "The LORD is gracious and compassionate, slow to anger and rich in love."[302]

> "The LORD is good to all; he has compassion on all he has made."[303]

"For the LORD your God is God of gods and Lord of lords, the great God, mighty and awesome, who shows no partiality and accepts no bribes."[304]

"He defends the cause of the fatherless and the widow, and loves the alien, giving him food and clothing."[305]

"The Most High . . . is kind to the ungrateful and wicked."[306]

"You do not stay angry forever, but delight to show mercy."[307]

"The Father of compassion and the God of all comfort."[308]

"For men are not cast off by the Lord forever. Though he brings grief, he will show compassion, so great is his unfailing love."[309]

"For God does not show favoritism."[310]

The Bible actually defines what love is.[311] Two of its central features are that love suffers long and is kind. And love never fails.

In Psalm 136, we're told to give thanks to the LORD, for He is good. Then the refrain,

His love endures forever . . .

His love endures forever . . .

His love endures forever . . .

His love endures forever . . .

His love endures forever . . .

is repeated 26 times for emphasis!

God's judgments are real!

Because punishment in hell is not endless does not mean that God's judgments are not real.

The question often comes up,

"What about Adolf Hitler . . . or Josef Stalin . . . or Chairman Mao? Or more recently, Saddam Hussein . . . or Osama bin Laden?"

Or what about those who have raped and abused defenseless women and children? Do they receive a "Get Out of Jail Free" card that keeps them in the game even after committing such gross atrocities?

No, they don't!

Believing that God will ultimately restore all of creation does not mean that wickedness is not judged. It does not mean that those who commit wicked deeds are not punished. It does not mean that after-death punishment is not both severe and intense for those who turn their backs on God's grace.

"The haughty looks of man shall be brought low, and the lofty pride of men shall be humbled . . . For the LORD of hosts has a day against all that is proud and lofty, against all that is lifted up – and it shall be brought low."[312]

"Do not be deceived: God is not mocked, for whatever one sows, that will he also reap."[313]

"I will punish the world for its evil, the wicked for their sins."[314]

"I will put an end to the arrogance of the haughty and will humble the pride of the ruthless."[315]

"God opposes the proud."[316]

"God is a consuming fire."[317]

"It is a fearful thing to fall into the hands of the living God."[318]

The Judge of all the earth will judge sin. The God of heaven does mete out punishment. Sometimes very severe and sometimes very long. Sometimes in this age and sometimes in the age or ages to come. Jesus Himself when referring to future punishment explained that some will be beaten with many blows, while others will be beaten with few blows.[319]

But God's judgments go beyond simply punishing sin. The apostle Paul called himself the worst of sinners.[320] And he wasn't speaking out of false modesty. He had intentionally persecuted, and even had Christians put to death. But God didn't just punish Paul for his sins. He didn't just prevent him from doing bad things. God transformed Paul's heart so that Paul became a powerful force for doing good.

Hitler, Stalin, Mao, Hussein, bin Laden and others who have done truly wicked things will be punished. They don't just get a light tap on the wrist and a free pass to heaven. But ultimately, God's intent is not to punish. It is to transform.

The Scriptures are very clear that God is both all-powerful and all-loving. Those who believe in ultimate restoration see those two qualities working together through the ages to accomplish God's good purposes. It's those who believe in endless punishment who see some kind of division within God's nature. But that division is artificial. It doesn't exist.

There's no internal conflict within God.

Grace in time of need

"Thank you, Pastor," she said with tears in her eyes.

"Your words have encouraged my heart!"

He carefully took her hand in his and responded kindly.

"I'm so glad to hear that. If there's anything I've learned in my years of ministry, it's that God is much more gracious than most people think."

Chapter 12

But what about . . . ?

"There's something I don't understand, Mike," said a woman in our small adult Sunday School class. *"How can the Apostle Paul say that Abraham never doubted, when it's clear in the situation with Hagar that he definitely did doubt . . . in a very obvious way?"*

Mike was the class teacher. He'd gone to a Bible college and was very knowledgeable about his faith. I had often looked to him for answers to puzzling questions.

"You know," Mike said, *"I really don't have an answer for that. In fact, I've wondered about it myself. So let's take a look at what the Bible actually says and see what we can learn."*

I didn't envy Mike. The Genesis 16 account of how Abraham conceived a child with his wife's maidservant, Hagar, shows that Abraham did waver in his faith. He didn't really trust God to give him a child through his wife, Sarah, like God had promised. I didn't have a good answer for the woman's question, and Mike had just said that he didn't either.

I turned to the book of Romans, chapter 4, hoping to find that Paul didn't really say what I thought he said. But there it was in black and white. Abraham *". . . did not waver through unbelief regarding the promise of God . . ."*[821]

"Hmm," said Mike. *"Isn't that interesting? In the verse right before Paul's comment, he tells us what he's referring to, 'Without weakening in his faith, Abraham faced the fact that his body was as good as dead – since he was about a hundred years old.'"*[822]

Mike continued, *"The incident with Hagar happened when Abraham was in his eighties. Paul is talking about a much later time when Abraham was about a hundred. It was then that he didn't doubt God's promise. Paul is referring to a totally different situation."*

Wow! Mike answered the question by looking carefully at what the text actually said and putting the comments in the proper perspective.

The woman's question had nothing to do with heaven and hell, nor did the discussion that followed it. But I learned two very important lessons from that class about doing research.

First, always look at the context.

And second, don't give up looking for answers until you find one that makes sense.

Honest questions

Just because the Bible doesn't directly teach endless punishment doesn't mean that it isn't taught indirectly, especially if we're not careful to look at the context.

For example, what about the unpardonable sin? Or the comments by Jesus about forfeiting one's soul? Don't those passages indicate that some people will be separated from God forever?

Didn't Jesus say it would be better for Judas if he had never been born? How could that possibly be true if someday Judas is restored to fellowship with God?

And what about the impact of belief in ultimate restoration on Missions? Won't telling people that all will eventually be saved undermine efforts to spread the Gospel throughout the world?

These are important questions. So let's take a look at them.

The unpardonable sin

One of the greatest fears of Christians down through the centuries is that they've somehow committed the unpardonable sin, a sin so serious that it could never be forgiven. It's led some people to depression and despair, and caused others to give up. It's been the reason behind some people abandoning faith and morality because there's nothing left to lose.

While Bible teachers might agree that most people who express this concern have probably not committed such a sin, it's possible that some have. And if a sin is *unpardonable,* how can it be pardoned?

The fear actually stems from the words of Jesus Himself. He says that blaspheming the Holy Spirit is a sin that will not be forgiven.[323]

Jesus made His comment when He healed a demon-possessed man who could neither see nor speak. The common people were amazed and wondered if Jesus could be the promised Son of David. But instead of seeing what Jesus did as a true miracle of God, some of the religious leaders accused Him of being possessed by the devil, having an unclean spirit, and driving out demons by using the power of the devil himself.

The book of Mark records Jesus' response with these

words,

> "I tell you the truth, all the sins and blasphemies of men will be forgiven them. But whoever blasphemes against the Holy Spirit will never be forgiven; he is guilty of an eternal sin."[324]

Those are strong words. And they definitely give the impression that whoever commits this sin is in very great danger.

In order to get a better idea of what He meant when He said this, it's important to note that the word *never* in this passage is not in the Greek text. Jesus did not say the person will *never* be forgiven. He actually said that whoever blasphemes against the Holy Spirit will not be forgiven *to the age.* Or as it reads in Matthew, *"either in this age or in the age to come."*

Blasphemy against the Holy Spirit is refusing to acknowledge that what God is doing is really from God. It's resisting His work in our lives. It's saying no to Him. As long as that continues, nothing can be done. It's impossible for someone to experience God's forgiving grace when that person doesn't want it, whether it takes place in this age, the age to come, or in one of the ages to come.

However, if after-death punishment is a place for healing sinners, when that is accomplished and they stop resisting God in their lives, then God's forgiveness is granted and heaven's doors are opened.

George MacDonald addressed this situation in his *Unspoken Sermon* on Light.

> "For the man who in this world resists to the full, there may be, perhaps, a whole age or era in the history of the universe during which his sin shall not be forgiven . . . How can they who will not repent be forgiven, save in the sense that

God does and will do all he can to make them repent? Who knows but such sin may need for its cure the continuous punishment of an æon?"[325]

God doesn't act graciously toward His creatures only in this age or in the age to come. According to the Apostle Paul, the incomparable riches of God's grace will be shown in the *ages* to come. [326]

God doesn't give up!

Forfeiting your soul

One of the best known tales in English literature is *The Tragic History of Dr. Faustus* by Christopher Marlowe.

It's based on the German legend of a successful scholar who was dissatisfied with his life and decides to make a deal with the devil. He sells his soul in exchange for unlimited knowledge and worldly pleasure.

For a period of time, Dr. Faustus experiences power and earthly delights beyond his wildest dreams. But in the end, his time runs out and the exchange takes place. He's damned forever. He gained for a moment what was valuable in this world, but lost for eternity what was valuable in the world to come. The story is definitely tragic.

Is that the kind of exchange Jesus is talking about when he asks,

> "What good will it be for a man if he gains the whole world, yet forfeits his soul? Or what can a man give in exchange for his soul?"[327]

Doesn't Jesus' comment here indicate that some people will forfeit their immortal souls and experience endless torment in hell because of it? Aren't they in essence making the same deal that Dr. Faustus made?

No, they're not.

Jesus made this statement while talking to His disciples immediately after predicting His upcoming death and resurrection.

In the verse just before this one, He tells them that anyone who wants to be His disciple must deny himself, take up his cross and follow Him. He then says that whoever wants to save his *life* will lose it, but whoever loses his *life* for Jesus' sake will find it.

The Greek word that's translated as *life* in that sentence is the same word that's translated as *soul* in the verse we're looking at. Translating the word differently in the two connected sentences gives the mistaken impression that Jesus is talking about two different things – one's *life* on earth on one hand, and one's eternal *soul* on the other. But He's not.

Jesus is *not* speaking about gaining or losing one's eternal soul in this passage. He's talking about the cost of being one of His followers here and now. Those who pursue their own agendas instead of following Him may gain earthly riches and honor, but they will lose the truly meaningful and purposeful life for which they were created.

Just after writing that paragraph, I saw this sign in the subway in New York City.

> "Sometimes when people get what they want,
> they realize how limited their goals are."

That phrase actually captures the essence of what Jesus is saying here. Those who pursue worldly power and delights in this life instead of indentifying with Christ are short-sighted, not realizing that in the end they've wasted their lives on things that are trivial.

Perish

It's been called the *Gospel in a nutshell*. The reference is short and can be written easily in inconspicuous places.

The In-N-Out Burger chain prints it on the inside bottom rim of their paper cups. The clothing chain Forever 21 prints it on the bottom of their shopping bags.

NFL football player and Heisman Trophy winner, Tim Tebow, printed it on his eye black. On January 8, 2012, Tebow threw 316 yards in a playoff upset against the Pittsburgh Steelers that became known as *The 3:16 Game*. After the game, John 3:16 became the top Google search in the US. It's one of the best known and most widely quoted verses in the entire Bible.

> "For God so loved the world that he gave his
> one and only Son, that whoever believes in him
> shall not perish but have eternal life."

Doesn't *perish* in this verse clearly mean that some will forever be excluded from the presence of God and the eternal life that He grants?

Again, the answer is no.

People often assume that when the Bible talks about perishing, it always relates to the immortal soul. But that is not correct. *Perish* simply means *to die*.[328] The idea is not extinction, but *ruin, loss – not of being, but of well-being*.[329]

You see this in the parable about pouring new wine into old wineskins. Jesus explained that if this is done, the new wine will burst the skins, the wine will run out and the wineskins will be ruined. The word He used is the same word we're talking about. He literally says that the wineskins will *perish*.[330]

That same word is also used to refer to the one *lost* sheep out of a hundred,[331] the Prodigal Son who was lost,[332] and the lost sheep of Israel that Jesus commanded His disciples to preach to. In each case, the lost items are said to have *perished*.[333] In reality, they hadn't yet been found.

When Jesus spoke to the crowd who saw Him multiply

the loaves and fish, He told them, *"Do not work for food that spoils."*[834] He literally told them not to labor for the food that *perishes.*

In John 3:16, Jesus is saying that those who believe in Christ now will not die in their sins but will have eternal life. Those who do not believe will die in their sins and face judgment before God and Christ.

But nothing in the passage, and nothing inherent in the meaning of the word *perish,* says anything about the nature or length of after-death punishment. Remember, the eternal life that Jesus promises in this verse to those who believe in Him is not something that relates only to the future.

It's what believers possess here and now.

The narrow door

When I took my survey in front of the New York Public Library and asked what percentage of the earth's population people believed will ultimately be in Heaven, I wanted to get a clear idea of what the average person on the street really thought, since death is the only thing we can really be sure of in life.

Jesus was once asked a very similar question.

"Lord, are only a few people going to be saved?"[335]

He answered with a parable to encourage His listeners to make every effort to enter through the *narrow door.*

Once the door is closed, many will try to enter but will be unable. They will knock and plead, but won't be let in. The result will be *"weeping and gnashing of teeth"* when they see Abraham, Isaac, Jacob and all the prophets sitting at a feast in the kingdom of God, but they themselves are thrown out.[336]

Doesn't Jesus' response clearly indicate that only a few

will go to heaven?

Unfortunately, the question phrased in most English versions gives a completely different sense from the question that was actually asked. The wording in the original Greek is,

> "Lord, are they few in number, those who are being saved?"[337]

It's a question about the number of people *at that time* who were accepting the message that Jesus brought. It wasn't a question about how many people would ultimately be saved, but how many people were *then* being saved. The kingdom of God is not only a future reality. It's a kingdom that Jesus was beginning to establish while He was here on earth.

Similarly, in the Sermon on the Mount, Jesus encouraged those in His audience to

> "Enter through the narrow gate. For wide is the gate and broad is the road that leads to destruction, and many enter through it. But small is the gate and narrow the road that leads to life, and only a few find it."[338]

As with many places where Jesus talks about life, He was not addressing the issue of the afterlife in this passage.

Jesus was telling His followers that the way to find the truly meaningful life that God desires us to have is actually found by comparatively few people. By contrast, there are many unproductive avenues in life that are broad, easy to follow and well traveled.

You simply need to look around at all the trivial things people pursue – the biggest house, newest car, whitest teeth, most Facebook friends, latest iPhone – to see the truth of that statement.

Jacob I loved, Esau I hated

My parents didn't treat my brother and me the same because we were different. We had different personalities, different interests, and different skills and abilities.

At times, when my mom would make something special for my brother, I would tease her by saying, *"You always did love Brian more than me!"* I could say that because she and I both knew that it was definitely not true. She and my dad loved us both with the same quality of love. It was a love that always had our ultimate best interests in mind, even though we were different.

There are very few things that I can think of that would be more disheartening than believing that my parents showed favoritism. And yet, that is what an often referred to passage in the Bible seems to be saying about God – that He deliberately chooses to extend His love and grace to some of those He created, while intentionally withholding it from the rest.

In the book of Romans, Paul says that God *loved* Jacob, but *hated* Esau.[339]

He then seems to justify the morality of this decision by explaining that God is a Potter who has the right to make out of the same lump of clay, some pottery for *noble* purposes and some for *common* use. Paul even says that some people are "objects of his wrath – prepared for destruction?"[340]

Don't these passages clearly say that God has favorites? That He hates and rejects some people, Esau at least. And that He prepares them for wrath and eternal damnation?

That's what many people think. In fact, it's often quoted as clear evidence that God has selected some people for salvation and others for eternal punishment.

But that is not what Paul is saying here. The passage is

definitely referring to God's sovereign purpose in choosing some and not others. But Paul is not referring to selection for salvation. Rather, he is referring to God's selection for service – those chosen to be His instruments.

It's also important to note that the reference is to the Old Testament book of Malachi where it is generally understood to be referring to the descendants of Jacob and Esau – the nation of Israel and the Edomites – not to Jacob and Esau themselves.[341]

The true intent of God's comment is consistent with the Hebrew use of exaggeration to make a point.[342] This occurs many times in both the Old and New Testaments. For example, Job says

"my path was drenched with cream and the rock poured out for me streams of olive oil."[343]

What Job meant was that he had an abundance of good things.

When the Israelite spies came back from going through the promised land of Canaan to see what it was like, they told the people

"the cities are large, with walls up to the sky."[344]

It was their way of saying that the walls were very high.

We often do the same thing when we tell our friends that *it's raining cats and dogs.* Or, *I've fallen head over heels in love.* Or, *that dessert is to die for!*

Jesus Himself illustrated this when He said,

"If anyone comes to me and does not hate his father and mother, his wife and children, his brothers and sisters – yes, even his own life – he cannot be my disciple."[345]

He obviously didn't mean we should literally hate our parents, wives, siblings and children. That would require us to violate the Biblical commands to honor our parents, love our wives and children, and love our neighbors as ourselves. He meant that parental, spousal and brotherly love must take second place to love for Him.

In a similar way, God is saying that Esau must take second place to Jacob, even though that was contrary to the custom of the day relating to inheritance rights. Although Jacob was the second born son, God gave the first-born rights to Jacob's descendants in order to fulfill the blessing given to Abraham.

But that decision does not mean that Esau and his descendants are irrevocably rejected and destined for eternal suffering in hell. It simply means that they were not the ones God chose to use to fulfill His promise to Abraham, that through him all nations would be blessed.

Paul says that God's plan has always been to choose some for service and not others. But His purpose has always been to show mercy and compassion.[346]

As a Potter, God certainly has the right to fashion out of the same lump of clay, some vessels for *honorable* use and some for *common* use. But being made for common use does not imply that those vessels are eternally rejected and cursed. They were simply not chosen for a special, honorable purpose.

Ishmael, Esau and most of the Jews of Paul's day were not chosen to experience the honor of serving as God's chosen vessels to bring about the fulfillment of His promise. That honor went to a remnant of the Jews and the believing Gentiles in accordance with God's plan.

The objects of *wrath* that Paul mentions are those who actually became objects of His *mercy*. As he wrote to the believers in Ephesus,

> "Like the rest, we were by nature objects of wrath. But because of his great love for us, God, who is rich in mercy, made us alive with

Christ even when we were dead in
transgressions . . ."[347]

Paul himself was once an object of wrath who later
became an object of mercy. Assuming that you are now a
true believer in Christ, so were you. And so was I.[348]

Paul concludes this section of his book by saying that
"God has bound all men over to disobedience
so that he may have mercy on them all."[349]

Rather than saying that God has rejected some of those
He created and predestined them to never-ending
suffering, Paul is actually explaining that God has not
rejected any of those He created. He is merciful to both
Jews and Gentiles.

Paul is not talking about sending people to eternal
torment. He's talking about God's plan to show mercy to
all.

God hardened Pharaoh's heart

What comes to your mind when you hear about a
hardened criminal? If you're like most of us, you think of
someone who is confirmed in the error of his ways and will
never change. He has chosen the wrong path, and no
matter what is done to help him he will continue in it.

Did God actually cause Pharaoh to be hardened in the
error of his ways? That seems to be what Moses says in
the book of Exodus, and Paul seems to confirm it in the
book of Romans. If that's true, then Pharaoh will never
repent, and certainly be in danger of experiencing never-
ending punishment.

But it's not true.

The Bible does say that God hardened Pharaoh's heart.
But it was not to keep him from knowing and experiencing
the truth of God's saving power.

When Moses first came to Pharaoh to ask him to release the Israelites from their bondage, Pharaoh responded by saying that he didn't *know* the God Moses was talking about.[350] He and the Egyptians worshipped a lot of gods, but they didn't know the one true God. The plagues that came on Egypt were designed to reveal to Pharaoh and his people who the true God is, and show them that the idols they worshipped had no real power.

The words translated *hardened* in reference to Pharaoh also mean to *make firm*.[351] In fact, it's the same word that God used when He told Joshua to be strong and courageous.

God made Pharaoh's heart firm so he would not buckle under the immense pressure that would come on him when God's power was being demonstrated. As a result, God was able to fully display His supremacy over the false gods of Egypt and reveal to Pharaoh and all the Egyptians who He really was – the true Ruler and Savior of all the earth.

The hardening God brought on Pharaoh did not make him unable to repent or keep him from salvation. That's clear from the fact that the hearts of Pharaoh's servants were also hardened. But they later acknowledged that they'd been wrong and urged Pharaoh to let the people go.[352]

God made Pharaoh's heart firm so His power to save could be seen by all – including Pharaoh and the Egyptians. As He said to Moses,

> ". . . the Egyptians will know that I am the LORD when I stretch out my hand against Egypt and bring the Israelites out of it."[353]

Let him be eternally condemned

It's not surprising to hear people say to someone they're fed up with, *"Go to hell!"*

In most English versions of Galatians 1:8-9, Paul seems to say exactly that about those who preached a different message than he did. In fact, he says it twice.

> "But even if we or an angel from heaven should preach a gospel other than the one we preached to you, let him be eternally condemned! As we have already said, so now I say again: If anybody is preaching to you a gospel other than what you accepted, let him be_eternally condemned!"

He may not be using street language, but Paul definitely seems to be saying that those who disagree with him will be condemned forever. And where else would that be but in hell?

The word translated *eternally condemned* is *anathema* in Greek. It's the same word that Paul uses in a passage in Romans when he expresses his great desire to see his fellow Jews restored to a good relationship with God. There he says,

> "I could wish that I myself were cursed (*anathema*) and cut off from Christ for the sake of my brothers, those of my own race, the people of Israel."[354]

Anathema is frequently used in the Greek translation of the Old Testament to refer to something devoted to God. It's sometimes used to mean things devoted for His service, as with sacrifices or gifts offered up to God. And it's also used for people or things that are to be devoted to destruction, like an idol or a city that was to be destroyed. In the New Testament, it acquired the more general meaning of *God's disfavor*.

In the passage in Galatians, Paul uses *anathema* to refer to those who preach a false gospel. In Romans, it refers to Paul himself. The controlling thought in both passages is delivering someone into God's hands for His judgment.[355]

Preaching a false message about Christ is serious. Paul's words are very strong. But nothing in the word *anathema* indicates that the punishment someone experiences at the hand of God is to go on forever. Paul isn't consigning his enemies to eternal damnation. He's simply turning them over to God.

In the Old Testament book of Ezekiel, God says,

> "I take no pleasure in the death of the wicked, but rather that they turn from their ways and live. . . . if I say to the wicked man, 'You will surely die,' but he then turns away from his sin and does what is just and right . . . he will surely live; he will not die."[356]

The curse that Paul is asking to be placed on ungodly people is that they experience God's hand of judgment . . . until they recognize their error and turn from it.

Repentance is impossible

One of the most often asked questions about heaven and hell might be stated as a riddle:

> "How far back can a backslider slide before a backslider can't slide back?"

Many have suggested that the answer is found in the book of Hebrews.

> "It is impossible for those who have once been enlightened, who have tasted the heavenly gift, who have shared in the Holy Spirit, who have tasted the goodness of the word of God and the powers of the coming age, if they fall away, to be brought back to repentance, because to their loss they are crucifying the son of God all over again and subjecting him to public

disgrace."[357]

If it's *impossible* for someone who's fallen away to be brought back to repentance, isn't it clear that they will never enter the presence of God? If it's impossible for them to enter heaven, where else could they be but in hell?

The writer of the book of Hebrews is talking to people who were slow to learn.

By this time, they should have been teachers themselves, but instead they needed others to teach them.[358] As with many people today, these teachers were stuck going over and over the same things with people who were really only interested in arguing, not in learning the truth.

The word *impossible* here has a force similar to what Jesus said to His disciples after He told them it would be easier for a camel to go through the eye of a needle than for a rich man to enter the kingdom of God. Again, notice the use of exaggeration to make a point.

The disciples were

> "greatly astonished and asked, 'Who then can be saved?' Jesus looked at them and said, 'With man this is impossible, but with God all things are possible.'"[359]

The writer of Hebrews is not saying that it's impossible for *God* to bring someone who's fallen away from the faith back to repentance. Rather, it's impossible, and a waste of time, for Christian leaders to try to reconvert someone who's been acquainted with all the proofs and elements of Christianity and chosen to abandon them.

This would seem to apply to Peter, and it certainly may have been on Peter's mind after he denied Christ three times. He had

> "once been enlightened ... tasted the heavenly gift ... shared in the Holy Spirit ... tasted the

goodness of the word of God and the powers
of the coming age ... fallen away and subjected
Jesus to public disgrace."[360]

The other disciples undoubtedly tried to restore Peter
with their words. However, it was not until Jesus Himself
came and spoke directly to Peter, asking him three times if
he loved Him, that Peter was restored.

With God at work in people's lives through the ages, the
answer to the above riddle is actually the same one that
would have been given by the Prodigal Son's father.

"He can slide as far back as a backslider slides
until the backslider turns to slide back!"

The Lake of Fire

The book of Revelation is a fascinating book, filled with
graphic imagery of God's final judgment and the
establishment of His kingdom. The images are so striking
that they've become the source for artists and writers
throughout the centuries who've sought to portray what
endless punishment in hell will be like.

What people often fail to notice is that the plagues,
earthquakes, famines, and other calamities mentioned in
Revelation all occur *on earth* before the final judgment.
They don't picture what goes on in hell *after* death. They
picture what happens on earth *before* death.

One image, however, does relate directly to the fate of
the wicked after death. The wicked will be cast into the
Lake of Fire.[361]

"the cowardly, the unbelieving, the vile, the
murderers, the sexually immoral, those who
practice magic arts, the idolaters and all liars –
their place will be in the fiery lake of burning
sulfur. This is the second death."[362]

We're also informed that the devil, the beast and the false prophet are there, and they will be *tormented day and night forever and ever* – or as we saw earlier, for *ages of ages.*[363]

That definitely sounds like something horrendous beyond description in the English translations. But the words in their original language give a much different picture of what the purpose of the Lake of Fire really is.

The word translated *sulfur* originally referred to fire from heaven.

It's connected with sulfur because it was used in pagan religious rites for *purification.*[364] Pre-Roman civilizations used it as a medicine, a fumigant, a bleaching agent and in incense. And the Romans used sulfur or fumes from its combustion as an insecticide, and to purify a sick room to cleanse its air of evil.[365]

The term translated *torment* originally referred to the action of an inspector who sought to test the quality of gold and silver coins. In its proper sense it is a means of testing and proving.[366]

For the apostle John who authored the book of Revelation, and for his readers in the ancient world, the Lake of Fire was not a place of unending torture. It was not a place with no purpose other than to inflict pain. It was a *refiner's* fire. Its purpose was to purify and cleanse from evil in the age to come. God is good. His punishments have a good purpose.

The Book of Life

After paying for and helping plan my oldest daughter's wedding, I quickly came to the conclusion that I would never again question why I was or was not invited to someone else's wedding reception. So many factors go into preparing a guest list.

"We just have to invite this person! We really

want these people – is there any way we can possibly fit them in? I honestly wish we could invite them, but there's no room . . . or we can't afford it . . . or . . ."

If you're fortunate enough to get an invitation, it's not unusual to see a table with name cards neatly laid out so guests can quickly locate where they will be sitting. Sometimes, there's a large, beautifully bound book on the table listing the invited guests in alphabetical order, with a well-dressed young man or woman standing beside it to help you see if your name is written there.

The Bible talks of a similar book – the Book of Life – that contains a limited list of the names of those who will ultimately be allowed into the presence of God.[367] Those whose names are not written in this book will be thrown into the Lake of Fire.[368]

That's about as clear a statement as you can get to say that some people *will*, and some people *will not* get into heaven. So even if the Lake of Fire is in some way temporary and has a refining purpose, how can those whose names are not listed in the Book of Life get their names listed there – especially after they've literally been through hell?

The answer to this dilemma lies in understanding what names are actually written in the Book of Life. For example, is Abram written there . . . or is it Abraham? Is Saul of Tarsus written in the book . . . or is it Paul the apostle?

The Bible is clear that those who are able to enter into God's presence are those who have been *born again*.[369] They are a new creation. Old things have passed away. All things have become new.[370]

In Revelation 2:17, Jesus tells those who need to turn from their sinful ways that if they do so, He will give them "a white stone, with a new name written on the stone that no one knows except the one who receives it."

The Book of Life lists the names of all those who will be allowed into the presence of God. It's a fixed list with no new names added to it. But people can – as all those who turn to Christ do, whether in this age or in an age to come – receive a new name. It's that *new name* that's been written in the Book of Life from the beginning of time.

Better if Judas had not been born

I can't think of anything that would be more horrific than hearing Jesus Christ say that it would be better for me if I had never been born!

And yet those words, as translated in many of the most popular English versions of the Bible, are spoken by Jesus about Judas Iscariot, the disciple who betrayed Him.[371]

The words in both the Matthew 26:24 and Mark 14:21 passages are exactly the same.

> "The Son of Man goes as it is written of him, but woe to that man by whom the Son of Man is betrayed! It would have been better for that man if he had not been born."[372]

It certainly sounds like a fate worse than death! How can that possibly be reconciled with a belief in ultimate restoration?

Cursing the day of one's birth was actually a proverbial expression of overwhelming grief in ancient Judaism and another example of the use of exaggeration to make a point. [373]

The word *woe*, in both English and Greek, is primarily an expression of deep heartache and anguish.[374] It's grief. It's overwhelming sorrow.[375] It's a condition of deep

185

suffering.[376]   The synonym for woe is *sorrow,* not displeasure.

When Jesus said, *"Woe to that man . . ."* He was foreseeing that Judas, a disciple He had chosen and no doubt loved, would be overwhelmed with grief when he realized what he had done. The intent of His comment was not anger and displeasure. It was sadness of heart.

Jesus foresaw accurately what did, in fact, happen to Judas. A sense of overwhelming sadness came over him shortly after his betrayal.

> "When Judas, who had betrayed him, saw that Jesus was condemned, he was seized with remorse and returned the thirty silver coins to the chief priests and the elders. 'I have sinned,' he said, 'for I have betrayed innocent blood.'
>
> "'What is that to us?' they replied. 'That's your responsibility.'
>
> "So Judas threw the money into the temple and left. Then he went away and hanged himself."[377]

Jesus was deeply grieved that His disciple would experience profound sadness for betraying the one Person who had truly loved him. If Jesus' comment about Judas is translated correctly in the English versions, it may have been a cultural way of describing His deep sorrow over Judas' decision. Judas, in his own eyes, would certainly have felt that it would be good if he had never been born.

But the verse is not translated correctly in the English versions.

The verse talks of two people – the *Son of Man,* also referred to as *him . . .* and *Judas,* referred to as *that man.*

In Greek, Jesus says that it would be *good* (not better) for *him* if *that man* had not been born. But the English versions actually flip words around and say it's good for *that man* if *he* had not been born. This change clearly gives the impression that *Judas* is the only one being spoken about in the passage.

However, if Jesus' words were translated correctly, there would be no difficulty in understanding Him to mean that it would have been good for Jesus Himself if Judas had not been born.

> "The Son of Man indeed goes, as it has been written concerning him, but woe to that man (Judas) through whom the Son of Man is delivered up! It would be good for Him (the Son of Man) if that man (Judas) had not been born."[378]

In the discussion with the disciples about His upcoming betrayal, Jesus was clearly saddened about Judas. But His mind was also preparing for His own suffering. Humanly speaking, Jesus did not want to go to the cross and suffer an anguishing death.

In the Garden of Gethsemane, He prayed with great intensity that the cup of suffering He was about to experience would pass from Him. Luke says that He was in anguish, and His sweat was like drops of blood falling to the ground.[379]

In that context, Jesus was not saying that it would have been better for Judas if he had never been born. Rather, Jesus spoke of His grief concerning the disciple who was about to betray Him, and in the process expressed His desire that it would be good for Jesus if Judas had not been born.

What about missions?

Not long ago, I received a letter from a Christian missionary organization that addressed a primary reason people state for not believing in ultimate restoration. It's not a Biblical issue at all. It's a practical one.

The letter explained,

> "The work of missions is not a numbers game, but numbers don't lie. Statistically, in the time it probably took you to scan the envelope, open the letter, and read these first two sentences, 10 human beings died having never heard the good news about Jesus. Gone forever.
>
> "I'm told that about 150,000 people will die today! Nearly half of them will have never heard that Jesus came that they might have life. In fact, most of them live in places where they have no reasonable access to that truth . . . and our access to them is limited.
>
> "We can sensationalize the numbers, but people are not numbers. Jesus died for people, and as Dr. Henry said, 'The gospel is only good news if it gets there in time.'"

If everyone will eventually get into heaven anyway, why share your faith?

Why should missionaries and other Christians dedicate themselves to hard work, danger, suffering and possibly death – often in distant and backward lands – to tell others about the *Good News?*

And just as important, won't proclaiming the message of ultimate restoration strip the people back home of the motivation to donate the necessary finances to keep the work going?

First, the most important reason for telling people of God's ultimate victory over sin for all humanity is because it's true.

One of the distinctive teachings of Biblical Christianity is that the ends do *not* justify the means. Regardless of the results of our conduct or actions, we are to pursue truth wherever it leads. That's what the Early Church did. The greatest time of expansion for the Christian Church was in the first centuries after Christ, when a great many Christians and Christian leaders believed that God would ultimately restore all.

Second, God wants us to love Him with all our heart, all our soul, all our mind and all our strength. That is the first great commandment. But He also wants us to genuinely love people. The second great commandment is to love our neighbors as ourselves.

There are people hurting everywhere, and the message of God's redeeming love does much more than simply provide a fire insurance policy to keep people out of hell.

The apostle Paul explained that God was reconciling the world to himself in Christ.[380] Peter, when speaking to those who had witnessed the healing of a man crippled from birth, told them of God's purpose to bless people by *transforming* their lives.[381] Jesus came so people would have life, and have it to the full.[382] When people were hungry, He fed them. When they were sick, He healed them. When they had a spiritual need, He addressed and met that need.

As people find their place in God's plan for their lives, they will experience reconciliation with God and with others. They will experience forgiveness of their sins. They will experience power to overcome sinful habits. And they will experience true purpose. The result is the greatest joy and true fulfillment. That's why it's called *Good News!* And those who've experienced it for themselves will want to tell others.

A third reason we should share the message about ultimate restoration is because the traditional concept of hell is actually one of the greatest *hindrances* to spreading the faith.

People find it very difficult to believe that an all-powerful, all-loving God would consign people to endless, conscious suffering because they're not part of a special group, or because they've never responded positively to a message they've never heard.

Endless suffering is not good news.

That's especially true for people who've grown up in a non-Christian environment where the Christian message has rarely or never been heard. It's not good news to hear that virtually every ancestor, relative, friend or loved one who has died, and the vast majority of those still alive have no hope. It's not good news to be told that all or almost all of the people you love are suffering or will suffer endless torture at the hands of the God you're telling them about.

That's not the *greatest* news ever told. It's the most *dreadful* news!

That's one of the reasons why it's been so hard for the gospel to take root in cultures that place a high value on family relationships. The first Christian missionary to Japan, St. Francis Xavier, experienced this response to the message he preached in the year 1552.

> "One of the things that most of all pains and torments these Japanese is, that we teach them that the prison of hell is irrevocably shut, so that there is no egress therefrom. For they grieve over the fate of their departed children, of their parents and relatives, and they often show their grief by their tears.

> "So they ask us if there is any hope, any way to free them by prayer from that eternal misery, and I am obliged to answer that there is absolutely none. Their grief at this affects and torments them . . . they almost pine away with sorrow . . . They often ask if God cannot take

their fathers out of hell, and why their punishment must never have an end. . . .

"I can hardly restrain my tears sometimes at seeing men so dear to my heart suffer such intense pain about a thing which is already done with and can never be undone."[383]

I've served on the staffs of three Christian organizations directly involved in missionary activity and have been active in sharing my faith for most of my adult life. For the majority of that time, I've believed in God's ultimate victory over sin for all. Far from being a hindrance to me in sharing my faith, this belief has given me a freedom and confidence to talk very openly with people from almost every walk of life. It's enabled me to help a great many people.

In my experience, the doctrine of eternal damnation has caused far more people to be driven away from the faith than drawn to it.

My friend Diane summed up the answer to the question *What about missions?* very well.

"I used to be afraid to share the gospel, for fear that the conversation would come around to the subject of hell. I was afraid that someone would ask, "What about those who have never heard?" or "How can a good God allow billions of people to be tormented forever?" or "What's the point of bringing people into existence only to suffer in this life, die, and then suffer forever with no hope of relief?

"I had no good answers. Sure, I knew all the standard answers, but they didn't satisfy me any more than they satisfied those who asked the questions.

"Now I am free to share the gospel without worrying about getting trapped by good questions that have no good answers. I can confidently proclaim that God is Love, that He is not a monster who allows people to spend eternity in perpetual suffering apart from Him.

"At the same time, I can confidently proclaim that He is holy and righteous, He is a consuming fire, and He will not let anyone get away with anything. He will do whatever it takes to make sinners holy, fit for spending eternity in His presence."[384]

Honest answers

"The written assignment for this course will be a paper on a subject of your choosing. A written description of the paper will be due on February 20. The paper itself will be due on April 5. Please feel free to talk to me during office hours about possible subjects."

It was my last semester at seminary. I'd been wondering about endless suffering in hell for a long time. I didn't know what I would discover, but I wasn't satisfied with the answers I had heard or read. The lessons I learned a few years earlier in Mike's Sunday School class certainly seemed to apply here. This was an opportunity to look carefully at the subjects of heaven and hell to find an honest answer to an honest question.

"Thanks, Mike!"

Chapter 13

How wide are heaven's doors ... really?

"Daddy, can I talk to you for a minute?"

Long before I started writing this book, I was sitting in my office going through the mail when my youngest daughter walked in. She was 8 years old, and the look on her face told me something was wrong.

"Sure, sweetheart, what's the problem?"

"Well," she answered, *"I don't think some of my friends are going to heaven. I pray for them every night. If God doesn't answer my prayers, I'll be really sad."*

I motioned for her to come over and sit on my lap. I hugged her close, and said, *"You know something. I think you're right. It really would be sad if the people who are important to us never ended up in heaven. I don't tell this to too many people because it could cause some problems at the church. But I actually believe that God is going to get everyone into heaven someday."*

"Really?!"

"Yup. A long time ago, I asked the same question you're asking. And when I checked it out in the Bible, you know what?"

"What?"

"I discovered that the Bible actually teaches that someday all the people you love – and all the people who are loved by somebody else – will be there. You see, God is very good. And God is very powerful. He loves everybody. And in the end, everybody He loves will be with Him in heaven."

"Wow! That makes me happy. I hope you won't get in trouble for telling me."

"Don't worry, sweetheart. Someday I'm going to tell everyone!"

What do you believe?

I would love to continue giving more and more evidence that the all-powerful, all-loving God of the Bible has a bigger and better plan for us than we may have been led to believe.

In fact, if you have not already done so, let me encourage you to read through the additional information in the Endnotes in this book. There's a lot of interesting information there that you may find helpful and encouraging.

But if you've read this far, you've seen enough to at least question whether or not the God of the Bible would cause or allow a large part of His creation to suffer consciously in hell forever. Now it's time to take a quick look at some of the positive statements in Scripture that strongly suggest that He wouldn't.

The real story of Christmas

We sometimes overlook the message that is at the heart of Christianity.

Jesus Christ is the Savior of the world!

The angel who appeared to the shepherds on that glorious night to announce the birth of the promised Savior did *not* say, "I bring you good news of great joy that will be for *some* of the people," or even "for *most* of the people."

The angel said,

> "I bring you good news of great joy that will be for *all* the people."[385]

That's why it's good news. That's why it's good news of great joy. That's why a great company of the heavenly host appeared with the angel praising God. This was a message for all the people.

That message is confirmed by the best-known verse in the Bible.

> "For God so loved *the world* that He gave His only begotten Son . . . "[386]

The very next verse explains why Jesus came.

> ". . . that *the world* through him might be saved."[387]

It was made clear by John the Baptist when he revealed who Jesus was.

> "Behold, the Lamb of God who takes away the sin of *the world*."[388]

When speaking to the crowd after His triumphal entry into Jerusalem, Jesus said,

> "And I, when I am lifted up from the earth, will draw *all people* to myself."[389]

In His prayer in the Upper Room just before His crucifixion, Jesus said God had given Him authority over *everyone,* so that He could give eternal life to *everyone* God had given Him.[390]

In his first letter to Timothy, Paul said that God wants all people to be saved and come to a knowledge of the truth. This will happen because Christ Jesus

> "gave Himself as a ransom for *all people.*"[391]

Paul further explained that we've put our hope in the living God

> "who is the Savior of *all people*, and especially of those who believe."[392]

And John told his readers that Christ

> "is the atoning sacrifice for our sins, and not only for ours but also for the sins of the *whole world.*"[393]

The message at the heart of Christianity is that Jesus Christ came to redeem all mankind!

The real message of the Bible

One of the most common responses I get when I tell people that I believe everyone will someday be in heaven is, "I wish it were true, *but . . .*"

The *but* is usually followed by, "I have never heard that before! Where in the Bible does it say anything like that?"

Responding to those comments is really what this book is all about. But the short answer can be expressed rather simply. God is good!

His love is unconditional. His power is irresistible. And He never gives up.

That's why He didn't abandon Adam and Eve when they sinned in the Garden of Eden.[394] That's why He didn't abandon Israel when they turned away from Him to follow other gods.[395] That's why He won't abandon you . . . or me . . . or any of those He created.

God's love and faithfulness were communicated over and over throughout the Old Testament when the priests and the people praised the God of heaven:

"He is good; His love endures forever!"[396]

It's what God revealed to Moses when He showed him who He really is:

"the compassionate and gracious God, slow to anger and abounding in love and faithfulness . . . maintaining love to a thousand generations and forgiving wickedness, rebellion and sin!"[397]

It's what David understood, especially after he fell far short of being the man after God's own heart in the affair with Bathsheba, the wife of Uriah. David wrote in Psalm 102,

"He will not always accuse, nor will he harbor his anger forever; he does not treat us as our sins deserve or repay us according to our iniquities."[398]

Similarly, the prophet Micah ends his book with these words,

"You do not stay angry forever but delight to show mercy. You will again have compassion on us; you will tread our sins underfoot and hurl all our iniquities into the depths of the sea. You will be true to Jacob, and show mercy to Abraham, as you pledged on oath to our fathers in days long ago."[399]

It's what the prophets proclaimed as they looked to the distant future to see how God will treat the nations:

> "The LORD Almighty will prepare a feast of rich food for all peoples . . . he will destroy the shroud that enfolds all peoples, the sheet that covers all nations; he will swallow up death forever. The Sovereign LORD will wipe away the tears from all faces."[400]

Even Sodom, a city that had experienced punishment from which the imagery of hell was developed, isn't without hope of restoration. After telling Jerusalem that she not only walked in the ways of Sodom and Samaria, and became even more depraved than they, Ezekiel explained that God

> "will restore the fortunes of Sodom and her daughters and of Samaria and her daughters, and your fortunes along with them . . . And your sisters, Sodom with her daughters and Samaria with her daughters, will return to what they were before, and you and your daughters will return to what you were before."[401]

It's what the apostle Paul understood personally. He had persecuted Christians and even collaborated in their deaths. He knew that if God could save him, He could save everyone.

> "For as in Adam all die, so in Christ all will be made alive."[402]

How can this be? Paul's answer is clear.

> ". . . where sin increased, grace increased all the more."[403]

God's love

It's not uncommon to see a bumper sticker on a car or

graffiti on a wall that says, "God loves you." It's so common that it's almost become a cliché.

But is it true? Does God really love *you?*

The religious leaders of Jesus' day didn't think so. They thought God only loved people like them. So Jesus told them three parables to show them God's heart.

If a good shepherd has a hundred sheep and loses one, he's not satisfied to have 99% of the sheep in his possession. He wants all one hundred safely in the fold. So he searches *until* he finds what is lost.[404]

A woman had ten silver coins and lost one. She wasn't satisfied to have 90% of her wealth. Like the good shepherd, she searched carefully for what was lost *until* she found it.[405]

The last parable is the story of the Prodigal Son who took his inheritance, left for a distant country and squandered his wealth on wild living. The father knew that the consequences of his son's choices would eventually bring him to his senses. So he waited *until* his lost son returned after completely messing up his life. He welcomed him joyfully, and the son was restored.[406]

What did Jesus say about the extent of God's love?

He's not satisfied with the restoration of 50% . . . or 90% . . . or even 99% of what is His and what He loves. He seeks until He finds, and waits until the lost are found. He's not willing that any would remain forever separated from Him.

God's power

It's important to remember that God loves us unconditionally. But it's equally important to remember that God is the all-powerful Lord of all creation. He's the One with whom nothing is impossible. God accomplishes everything He intends to do.

Jesus said He came to seek and to save what was lost.[407]

Was He successful?

Before He was crucified, Jesus told a crowd that He would defeat the powers of darkness and in the process literally *drag* all people to Himself.[408]

Did He accomplish what He came to do?

The apostle Paul certainly thought He did. He had experienced God's power first-hand when Christ appeared to him on the road to Damascus. Paul bowed his knee before Him, and knew that one day

> ". . . every knee should bow, in heaven and on earth and under the earth, and every tongue confess that Jesus Christ is Lord, to the glory of God the Father."[409]

The most common explanation of this verse is that on Judgment Day God will force every tongue to confess that Jesus Christ is Lord. He'll be like the emperors in Rome who forced submission from their captives. But God is not a cruel tyrant who forces confessions from His vanquished enemies.

Scripture makes it clear that God does not look kindly on those who honor Him with their lips but not their hearts. Jesus challenged the Pharisees and teachers of the law who came to Him from Jerusalem with these words,

> *"You hypocrites! Isaiah was right when he prophesied about you: 'These people honor me with their lips, but their hearts are far from me. They worship me in vain . . .'"*[410]

The bowing before Him and confessing that Jesus is Lord is to the glory of God. It is *freely* given. In fact, every use in the New Testament of the word translated *confess* in the above verse connotes a *voluntary* confession.[411]

In his letter to the Christians in Rome, Paul tells us who Christ died for – the *ungodly*.[412] He also makes clear when Christ died for them – while they were *still sinners*.[413] He explains that in the same way that death for *all mankind* resulted from Adam's sin, so also the gift of life for *all mankind* comes by grace through Jesus Christ.

> ". . . if the many died by the trespass of the one man, how much more did God's grace and the gift that came by the grace of the one man, Jesus Christ, overflow to the many! . . . just as one trespass resulted in condemnation for all people, so also one righteous act resulted in justification and life for all people. For just as through the disobedience of the one man the many were made sinners, so also through the obedience of the one man the many will be made righteous. . . where sin increased, grace increased all the more."[414]

All mankind has sinned. All mankind needs a Savior. And God will have mercy on all mankind.[415]

How can this be? Because God's grace is far greater than mankind's sin. God overcomes evil by transforming the hearts of evil-doers and ultimately making them into those who love goodness. And we are told to go and do likewise.

> "Do not be overcome by evil, but overcome evil with good."[416]

To his readers in Corinth, Paul explained that

> "God was reconciling the world to himself in Christ, not counting men's sins against them."[417]

And in his letter to the Colossians, he said that just as God *created* everything and everyone in heaven and on earth through Christ, so He will *reconcile to Himself* everything and everyone in heaven and on earth through Christ.[418]

When Peter and John healed a crippled beggar in Jerusalem, a large crowd of people came running to see what happened. Peter told them about the One in whose name the crippled man was healed. He urged his audience to turn to God, and said that Christ must remain in heaven

> "until the time comes for God to restore everything."[419]

When will this take place? God will bring unity to all things in heaven and on earth under Christ

> "when the times will have reached their fulfillment."[420]

It doesn't depend on the resistance of the one being pulled. It depends on the power of the one pulling.[421]

God never gives up!

The book of Revelation is the last book in the Bible, and in it we witness an amazing thing. Christ is the only One in heaven or on earth or under the earth who is found worthy to break the seals and open the scroll of the Book of Life. To paraphrase a popular saying, when that happens, all heaven breaks loose!

> "Then I heard every creature in heaven and on earth and under the earth and on the sea, and all that is in them, singing, 'To him who sits on the throne and to the Lamb be praise and honor and glory and power for ever and ever.'"[422]

Who was singing these praises?

Every creature.

Where were these beings from?

Everywhere in God's creation.

At the very end of the book, we learn of a glorious city that has come down from heaven, filled with beauty that is beyond description. What we find is that the gates of the city are *always* open. The fruit of the tree of life is *always* available. Its leaves are for the healing of the nations. And at that time, there will no longer be any curse.[423] Then Jesus Himself says,

> "Blessed are those who wash their robes, that they may have the right to the tree of life and may go through the gates into the city."[424]

So who are those outside the city who are invited to wash their robes and go through the gates into the city?[425]

They're the same ones who, just a few verses earlier, were said to have their place in the fiery lake of burning sulfur – the sexually immoral, the murderers, the idolaters. Like the Prodigal Son, they are living outside the blessing of their Father. Why? Because those who are ungodly and impure are not allowed to enter through any of the city's twelve gates while they remain in that state.

But God doesn't give up on them. In the New Jerusalem where all this takes place, an invitation is given,

> "The Spirit and the bride say, 'Come.'"[426]

The *bride* is the body of believers throughout history who are already in the New Jerusalem. They don't need to wash their robes and eat of the tree of life because they've already done so. They're already in the city. The Spirit and the bride are calling to those outside the gates.

> "And let him who hears say, "Come." Whoever is thirsty, let him come; and whoever wishes, let him take the free gift of the water of life."[427]

There's another story to be told

I started and ended each chapter of this book with a story to help set the tone for the information I wanted to share. But the proper ending for this chapter is a story that I can't write, because it's a story that involves *you.*

It's a story based on all the things that have happened in your life to make you the person you are today. The influence of family and friends. The influence of schools, churches and jobs. Even the influence of the media – television, movies, books, the internet. All these things and more have helped shape who you are and what you believe.

If you've read this far, I thank you. I know you've been given a lot of information that's probably new to you. But in truth, it's been available for as long as Christianity has been around.

Most of what you've read provides a different interpretation of what we've always been told. As much as I'd like to prove that this interpretation is the one everyone should believe, I know that's not going to happen. Religious leaders and scholars have been preaching a very different view for 1,500 years. And I doubt that will change overnight with the publication of one book.

What can change, though, is what you believe and how you express those beliefs.

If you found yourself thinking, "I didn't know that" or "that makes sense" . . . maybe that's enough to encourage you to think about it some more and maybe even talk to others about what you really believe.

Or maybe what you read just helped confirm what you've believed all along, but you just weren't sure it was okay to feel that way – that you and those you love can count on God to never let you down, even in the afterlife.

It's *your* story that's important right now. And you're the only one who can tell it.

A final word

The tea kettle had just started whistling when I walked into the kitchen. My daughter waited for a moment until it came to a full boil, poured the water into a cup and looked at me.

"Hi, dad. Want a cup of tea?"

"No thanks," I answered.

She was the middle child in the family and had a special place in my heart . . . just like each of my 5 children. But now she was no longer a child. She was an adult.

"Do you know who I love more than you?" I asked.

She smiled, and answered, *"Nobody . . . except God of course!"* Then she came over and gave me a big hug.

"You're so silly," she said. *"But you know what? I'm glad you always asked us those questions. They made me feel loved!"*

As my children were growing up, I asked them "important questions" countless times so they would know that I loved them *all the way up to the sky and back again,* more times than they could ever imagine.

I wanted them to know they were *priceless* creations who were worth more to me than anything anyone could ever offer. And I wanted them to know that *nobody* would ever be able to move them away from their place at the center of my heart.

I did that because I was convinced that is how God looks at me . . . and my children . . . and you!

Throughout this book I've tried to look honestly and carefully at the major historical and Biblical issues that relate directly to the concepts of heaven and hell. I personally have concluded that all the people God created will ultimately be in heaven.

Why? Because of who God is.

He's not partial – favoring some over others. He doesn't change – acting graciously toward sinners while they're alive on earth, but then withdrawing His hand of mercy at death. He's not cruel – able to save all, but choosing rather to consign most of the human race to endless, conscious suffering. And He's not weak – desiring to save all, but ultimately powerless to do so.

God is good! God is powerful! And God is loving!

Hell is real, but not forever. Jesus Christ succeeded in His mission to seek and save what was lost.

A happy ending?

I'm an eternal optimist.

No, I don't always see the glass half full instead of half empty. I understand that sometimes the glass is definitely half empty. What I mean is that at the end of time, when eternity really begins, I expect to see a full glass.

In the beginning, God created a marvelous universe that He said was *very good*. In His wisdom, He allowed evil to enter that very good creation and mar what He had made. But God didn't allow evil to remain forever a part of His creation. Through the cross of Jesus Christ, God defeated sin and death completely, and will one day restore all of His creation to the perfection He originally intended.

But that perfection will be more than the innocence found in the Garden of Eden.

Salvation is not simply returning things to where they started. It's bringing things to where they were intended to be. God didn't abandon His creatures when they chose to turn away from Him. He pursued them even in death.

When all is said and done, God will have used the forces of evil to accomplish something far greater than what would have been if He had never given us the freedom to choose between right and wrong.

When all is said and done, all those He created will have come to know in their experience the difference between good and evil . . . and will have freely chosen good.

When all is said and done, all those God created will walk through heaven's doors, and God will truly be *all in all.*[428]

After the restoration of all things, the final word will once again be,

> *"God saw all that He had made, and it was very good!"*[429]

Endnotes

The historical and Biblical information provided in this book is well-documented. For those who would like a deeper understanding of the extensive research that helped form the beliefs expressed in *Heaven's Doors*, the following notes provide additional material, details and resources for your study.

Preface

[1] Long after I wrote this, the person came up to say hello to me at a conference. It turned out that "he" is a "she."

Chapter 1 – How much are you worth?

[2] Edward Young, *Night Thoughts, the Last Day, Book III*, The Works of Edward Young, Vol. III, Printed for J. Dodsley, London, 1798, p. 30

Chapter 2 – What are we talking about anyway?

[3] A similar definition was used in a survey conducted by the Pew Forum on Religion and Public Life. They reported that 92% of adult Americans believe in God, 74% believe in heaven, but only 59% believe in hell, which they defined as the place *"where people who have led bad lives and die without being sorry are eternally*

punished."

A book comprised of essays by scholars who were defending the traditional view of hell defined their belief as *". . . everlasting conscious punishment away from the joyous presence of God."* – Christopher W. Morgan, Robert A. Peterson, *Hell Under Fire: Modern Scholarship Reinvents Eternal Punishment*, Zondervan, 2004, p. 12

[4] *". . . the interpretation of hell as eternal conscious punishment is the one most widely attested by the Church . . . We also recognize that it represents the classic, mainstream evangelical position."* – The Nature of Hell: A Report by the Evangelical Alliance Commission on Unity and Truth Among Evangelicals, Carlisle: Acute/Paternoster, 2000, p. 134

[5] That belief was supported in a recent book with contributions from a number of highly respected scholars. Their assumption that any view other than Endless Punishment has little Biblical support was prevalent in several of the articles. Unfortunately, they did not deal with, or even seem to be aware of, most of the key Biblical issues related to the subject. – cf. Robert Yarbrough, "Jesus on Hell" in *Hell Under Fire: Modern Scholarship Reinvents Eternal Punishment*, edited by Christopher W. Morgan & Robert A. Peterson, Zondervan, Grand Rapids, MI, 2004, pp. 67ff; and J.I. Packer, "Universalism" in the same volume, p. 174

[6] It should be noted that the idea of "double-predestination" – ie. that God predestines some to evil – was specifically disavowed by the Christian Church in the Canons of the Council of Orange in AD 529. In its conclusion, the council states: *"We not only do not believe that any are foreordained to evil by the power of God, but even state with utter abhorrence that if there are those who want to believe so evil a thing, they are anathema."* – https://www.ewtn.com/library/COUNCILS/ORANGE.HTM

[7] Jonathan Edwards, "The Eternity of Hell Torments" – 1750, http://www.jonathan-edwards.org/Eternity.html
[8] Charles H.Spurgeon, "Profit and Loss" – a sermon (92) delivered on Sunday evening, July 6, 1856 at Exeter Hall, Strand, http://www.spurgeon.org/sermons/0092.php

[9] Edward Beecher, *History of Opinions on the Scriptural Doctrine of Retribution*, D. Appleton and Company, New York, 1878, p. 297

[10] John Wenham, *Facing Hell: An Autobiography*, (London: Paternoster, 1998), 254

Chapter 3 – Where did endless punishment come from?

[11] Genesis 3:19

[12] Luke 17:22-37

[13] We forget sometimes just how important punishments on this earth really are. As a result, we tend to overlook that aspect of God's judgment and focus primarily on punishments that will come after death. But from God's perspective, we would be wise to consider the results of our actions here on earth. Otherwise, God wouldn't have used them for 4,000 years as His primary motivation for people to do good.

[14] The comment in Daniel 12:2 about the dead being awakened – *"some to everlasting life, others to shame and everlasting contempt"* – will be addressed in our discussion of *aion* and *aionios* in Chapter 10.

[15] Daniel J. Block, "The Old Testament on Hell" in *Hell Under Fire: Modern Scholarship Reinvents Eternal Punishment*, edited by Christopher W. Morgan & Robert A. Peterson, Zondervan, Grand Rapids, MI, 2004, p.58

[16] Future blessings for the righteous were definitely implied in the Old Testament. For example, Hebrews 11:13 tells us that Abel, Enoch, Noah and Abraham considered themselves aliens and strangers on earth. Verse 19 of the same chapter explains that Abraham believed that God was able to raise the dead. Joseph asked to have his bones taken back to the Promised Land when the children of Israel returned. Job expressed his confidence that, after his skin had been destroyed, he would yet, in his flesh, see God. Elijah was taken up by a whirlwind into heaven. In Psalm 16:10, David expressed his hope that God would not abandon him in his death. The Psalmist in Psalm 49:15 stated confidently that *"God will redeem my life from the grave; he will surely take me to himself."*

Interestingly, a custom in ancient Israel actually foreshadowed an ultimate restoration of all things. The Jubilee festival, which lasted a whole year and took place twice in a century at the end of a period of seven sevens of years, brought release from bondage to *everyone* in the land. The Israelites were told, *"Consecrate the fiftieth year and proclaim liberty throughout the land to all its inhabitants.* – Leviticus 25:10

During the Jubilee year, *all* landed property in Israel reverted to its original owners, *all* slaves were set free, and *all* debts were cancelled. It didn't prefigure what would happen at the end of an *"age,"* such as seven years, but what would happen at the end of an *"age of ages"* – after *"seven Sabbaths of years"* – or seven sevens. Isaiah alluded to this unique event when he predicted the work of the future Messiah (Isaiah 61:1-3, 11). And, Jesus, when He returned from being tempted by the devil, went into the synagogue in Nazareth and read from that specific passage in Isaiah to announce His purpose for coming – *". . . to proclaim freedom for the prisoners and recovery of sight for the blind, to release the oppressed, to proclaim the year of the Lord's favor"* – Luke 4:18-21.

Jesus came to release *all* from bondage to sin and death. The great Jubilee festival foreshadowed what He would ultimately do.

[17] 1190 BC–1077 BC

[18] Taylor Ray Ellison, *The Book of Caverns*, http://www.touregypt.net/featurestories/caverns.htm

[19] *The Descent of Ishtar to the Underworld*, translation by Stephanie Dalley, *Myths From Mesopotamia: Creation, The Flood, Gilgamesh and Others*, *Oxford World's Classics*, Oxford University Press, 1989, revised edition 2000, p.155

[20] Plato, *Phaedo*, 111c, 113d ff, http://www.theoi.com/Kosmos/Tartaros2.html

[21] Virgil, *The Aeneid*, Book VI, translated by John Dryden, http://classics.mit.edu/Virgil/aeneid.6.vi.html

[22] Wisdom of Solomon 3:4

[23] Wisdom of Solomon 3:10

[24] Book of Enoch 103:8

[25] Some suggest that the Sadducees were the religious conservatives and the Pharisees were the religious liberals. Cf. *Zondervan Illustrated Bible Backgrounds Commentary*, vol. 1, Zondervan, copyright 2002, p. 25. Regardless of their labels, the

religious and political views of these two groups were opposed to one another.

[26] Flavius Josephus, *Antiquities*, XVIII, 1:3, translated by William Whiston. The Greek phrase he uses here is *eirgmon aidion*, http://www.ccel.org/ccel/josephus/works/files/ant-18.htm

[27] Flavius Josephus, *War of the Jews*, II, 8:14, translated by William Whiston. The Greek phrase he uses here is *aidios timoria*, http://www.ccel.org/ccel/josephus/works/files/war-2.htm

[28] Flavius Josephus, *War of the Jews*, II, 8:11, translated by William Whiston. The Greek phrases he uses here are *timoria adialeipton* and *athanaton timorion*, http://www.ccel.org/ccel/josephus/works/files/war-2.htm

[29] Philo, *On Rewards and Punishments*, XII, 69-70. The Greek phrase he uses here is *thanaton athanaton, ateleutaton*

[30] Matthew 15:7-9

Chapter 4 – What did the Early Church teach?

[31] Edward Beecher, *History of Opinions on the Scriptural Doctrine of Retribution*, D. Appleton and Company, New York, 1878

[32] *Origen*, Encyclopedia Brittanica – http://www.britannica.com/EBchecked/topic/432455/Origen

[33] Edward Beecher, *History of Opinions on the Scriptural Doctrine of Retribution*, D. Appleton and Company, New York, 1878, p. 189ff

[34] Alexandria was the home of one of the greatest Christian theological schools during the era of the Early Church fathers. The school, called the Didascalium , was founded in AD 190 by a man named Pantaenus – a man of superior learning and abilities, a teacher and a missionary who was martyred for his faith in Christ. Nothing remains of his writings. He was succeeded by Clement, Origen and others who were strong believers in ultimate restoration.

[35] Kingsley, Charles, *"Alexandria and Her Schools,"* Lecture IV, Macmillan, Cambridge, 1854, pp. 1-2, PagebyPageBooks.com

[36] *"It is essential, certainly, that the providence which manages all, be both supreme and good. For it is the power of both that dispenses salvation – the one correcting by punishment, as supreme, the other showing kindness in the exercise of beneficence,*

as a benefactor." – Clement of Alexandria, *Stromata*, Book I, Chapter 27

[37] *"God's punishments are saving and disciplinary, leading to conversion, and choosing rather the repentance than the death of a sinner, and especially since souls, although darkened by passions, when released from their bodies, are able to perceive more clearly, because of their being no longer obstructed by the paltry flesh."* – Clement of Alexandria, *Stromata*, Book VI, chapter 6

[38] *". . . So I think it is demonstrated that the God being good, and the Lord powerful, they save with a righteousness and equality which extend to all that turn to Him, whether here or elsewhere. For it is not here alone that the active power of God is beforehand, but it is everywhere and is always at work."* – Clement of Alexandria, *Stromata*, Book VI, chapter 6

[39] Clement of Alexandria, *Stromata*, Book VII, Chapter 2

[40] Clement of Alexandria, *Stromata,* Book VII, Chapter 16

[41] John R. Sachs, *"Apocatastasis* in Patristic Theology." *Theological Studies.* Volume: 54. Issue: 4. 1993. pp. 617. (NOTE: *"Apocatastasis"* is the Greek word referring to the doctrine of ultimate restoration; "Patristic" is the Latin/German word referring to the teachings of the Early Church fathers up until the time of Augustine.)

[42] Origen's accomplishments as a scholar and student of the Old Testament were outstanding. His works include letters, treatises in dogmatic and practical theology, apologetics, exegesis, and textual criticism. One of his books, *Against Celsus,* is a long, closely reasoned work refuting the arguments advanced by an influential second-century philosopher in Alexandria who was a very serious critic of Christianity. – Cf. Schaff, Philip, *History of the Christian Church*, Vol. II, Grand Rapids, Eerdmans, 1950 (copyright 1910 by Charles Scribner's Sons), pp. 790,792

Contemporary commentator Brian E. Daley, SJ, the Catherine F. Husking Professor of Theology at Notre Dame University, considers Origen to be *"the first fully professional Christian thinker."*– Brian E. Daley, SJ, *The Hope of the Early Church*, Cambridge University Press, Cambridge, New York, Melbourne, 1991, p. 59

[43] *The Hexapla*

[44] John R. Sachs, "Apocatastasis in Patristic Theology." *Theological Studies*. Volume: 54. Issue: 4. 1993. pp. 617

[45] *"We think, indeed, that the goodness of God, through His Christ, may recall all His creatures to one end, even His enemies being conquered and subdued. For thus says holy Scripture, 'The LORD said to My Lord, Sit Thou at My right hand, until I make Thine enemies Thy footstool.' And if the meaning of the prophet's language here be less clear, we may ascertain it from the Apostle Paul, who speaks more openly, thus: 'For Christ must reign until He has put all enemies under His feet.' . . . What, then, is this 'putting under' by which all things must be made subject to Christ? I am of opinion that it is this very subjection by which we also wish to be subject to Him, by which the apostles also were subject, and all the saints who have been followers of Christ."* – Origen, *De Principiis*, Book I, chapter VI, 1

[46] Origen, *De Principiis*, Book III, chapter VI, 5

[47] Origen, *Contra Celsus*, Book IV, chapter XIII

[48] *" . . . how much more is it to be understood that God our Physician, desiring to remove the defects of our souls, which they had contracted from their different sins and crimes, should employ penal measures of this sort, and should apply even, in addition, the punishment of fire to those who have lost their soundness of mind!"* – Origen, *De Principiis*, Book II, chapter X, 6

[49] John R. Sachs, "Apocatastasis in Patristic Theology." *Theological Studies*. Volume: 54. Issue: 4. 1993. pp. 617

[50] *"These subjects, indeed, are treated by us with great solicitude and caution, in the manner rather of an investigation and discussion, than in that of fixed and certain decision."* – Origen, *De Principiis*, Book I, Chapter VI

[51] To put that into perspective, the United States is less than 250 years old. The condemnation of Origen was like someone in political authority today condemning John Adams or Thomas Jefferson, and saying their understanding of what the Declaration of Independence or the U.S. Constitution was intended to be was completely wrong.

[52] One of Justinian's greatest achievements was the uniform rewriting of Roman law, the *Corpus Juris Civilis*, which is still the basis of civil law in many modern states.

[53] http://www.metmuseum.org/toah/hd/just/hd_just.htm

[54] https://en.wikipedia.org/wiki/Justinian_I

[55] Brian E. Daley, SJ, *The Hope of the Early Church*, Cambridge University Press, Cambridge, New York, Melbourne, 1991, p. 190

[56] There is also a question about whether or not the council in question – the Fifth General Council – was even an official and authorized Council of the Church, since it was not attended by Pope Vigilius, the primary representative of the Western Church.

[57] Edward Beecher, *History of Opinions on the Scriptural Doctrine of Retribution*, D. Appleton and Company, New York, 1878, pp. 178, 286; Schaff, *History*, Vol. II, p. 612; Catholic Encyclopedia.

[58] https://en.wikipedia.org/wiki/Justinian_I.

[59] Cf. Brian E. Daley, "Apocatastasis," *Encyclopedia of Christian Theology*, Volume 1, edited by Jean-Yves Lacoste, translated by Antony Levi, CRC Press, 2004, p. 68

[60] Origen and Origenism, *New Advent*, http://www.newadvent.org/cathen/11306b.htm; Henry R. Percival, "Excursus to the Anathemas," *A select Library of the Nicene and Post-Nicene Fathers*, Vol. XIV

[61] Philip Schaff, *History of the Christian Church*, Vol. III, Grand Rapids, Eerdmans, 1950 (copyright 1910 by Charles Scribner's Sons), p. 698

[62] Rev. Alexander Roberts, DD, and James Donaldson, LLD, *Ante-Nicene Christian Library, Vol. XXIII, Origen Contra Celsum*, T & T /Clark, Edinburgh, 1872, p. xxxii

[63] Victory M. Rentel, *St. Gregory, Father of Fathers*, http://stgregs.info/stgregory.htm

[64] Hans Urs von Balthasar, *Dare We Hope "That All Men Be Saved"?* – Ignatius Press, San Francisco, 1988, p. 245

[65] *"First, he believed in it because of the character of God. 'Being good, God entertains pity for fallen man; being wise, he is not ignorant of the means for his recovery.' Second, he believed in it because of the nature of evil. Evil must in the end be moved out of existence, 'so that the absolutely non-existent should cease to be at all.' Evil is essentially negative and doomed to non-existence. Third,*

he believed in it because of the purpose of punishment. The purpose of punishment is always remedial. Its aim is 'to get the good separated from the evil and to attract it into the communion of blessedness.' Punishment will hurt, but it is like the fire which separates the alloy from the gold; it is like the surgery which removes the diseased thing; it is like the cautery which burns out that which cannot be removed any other way." – William Barclay, *A Spiritual Autobiography*, William B. Eerdmans Publishing Company, Grand Rapids, 1977, p. 65

[66] Gregory of Nyssa, *Catechetical Oration*, VIII

[67] Gregory of Nyssa, *Catechetical Oration*, XXXV

[68] Gregory of Nyssa, Sermon I Corinthians 15:28, *Documents in Early Christian Thought*, edited by Maurice Wiles & Mark Santer, Cambridge University Press, 1975, p. 257. *"The Apostle says the same thing more plainly when he indicates the final accord of the whole Universe with the Good: 'That' to Him 'every knee should bow, of things in heaven, and things in earth, and things under the earth: And that every tongue should confess that Jesus Christ is Lord, to the glory of God the Father.'"* – Gregory of Nyssa, *A Select Library of Nicene and Post Nicene Fathers*, Vol. V, Gregory of Nyssa: *Dogmatic Treatises, Etc.*, T&T Clark, Edinburgh, Wm. B. Eerdmans Publishing Company, Grand Rapids, MI. p. 120

[69] Gregory of Nyssa, *Catechetical Oration*, XXVI

[70] John R.Sachs, "Apocatastasis in Patristic Theology." *Theological Studies*. Volume: 54. Issue: 4. 1993. pp. 617

[71] Acts 11:25

[72] Cf. A. Harnack, "Diodorus," *New Schaff-Herzog Encyclopedia of Religious Knowledge*, Vol. VIII, p. 436

[73] Diodorus, from Assemani Bibliotheca Orientalis, tom. iii., part i., p. 324, quoted by Hosea Ballou 2nd, *Ancient History of Universalism, From the Time of the Apostles to the Fifth General Council*, Universalist Publishing House, Boston, 1885, p. 185

[74] Theodore was born c. AD 350 and died in AD 428.

[75] F.A. Sullivan, "Theodore of Mopsuestia," *New Catholic Encyclopedia*, Vol. XIV, New York, McGraw-Hill, 1967, p. 18

[76] Frederick Loofs, "Theodore of Mopsuestia," *The New Schaff-Herzog Encyclopedia*, Vol. XI, New York, Funk & Wagnalls Company, 1911, p. 320

[77] Theodore of Mopsuestia, from Book V, *De Creatura*, quoted by Edward Beecher, *History of Opinions on the Scriptural Doctrine of Retribution*, D. Appleton and Company, New York, 1878, pp. 222-223

[78] Theodore of Mopsuestia, from Book V, *De Creatura*, quoted by Edward Beecher, *History of Opinions on the Spiritual Doctrine of Retribution*, D. Appleton and Company, New York, 1878, pp. 223-224

[79] Theodore of Mopsuestia, from Assemani Bibliotheca Orientalis, tom. iii., par. i., p. 323, quoted by Hosea Ballou 2nd, *Ancient History of Universalism, From the Time of the Apostles to the Fifth General Council*, Universalist Publishing House, Boston, 1885, pp. 244-245.

Theodore went on to explain, *"For, He never would have said, 'until thou hast paid the uttermost farthing (Mat. 5:26),' unless we could be released from punishment, after having suffered adequately for sin; nor would He have said, 'he shall be beaten with many stripes,' and again, 'he shall be beaten with few stripes,' (Luke xii.47, 48), unless the punishment to be endured for sin will have an end."*

[80] *"If the rewards of eternity so far exceed good works and the brief period of life, ought not the punishments much more to be overcome by the divine mercy? God would not revive the wicked at the resurrection, if they must needs suffer only punishment without reformation."* – Theodore of Mopsuestia, quoted by August Neander, *General History of the Christian Religion and Church*, Vol. IV, translated from the German by Joseph Torrey, Henry G. Bohn, London, 1851, note p. 446

[81] Theodore was condemned for views relating to the Nestorian controversy. Nestorius and his followers had been excommunicated for holding that Christ existed in two persons instead of two natures. They denied the accusation. Nestorius refused to call Mary *"The Mother of God,"* preferring the title, *"The Mother of Christ."*

Interestingly, the differences between the Orthodox and Nestorian views on the nature of Christ were specifically addressed in a historic meeting between John Paul II, Bishop of Rome and Pope of the Catholic Church, and His Holiness Mar Dinkha IV, Catholicos-

Patriarch of the Assyrian Church of the East (the official name of the Nestorian Church) that occurred in November of 1994. A joint statement was issued explaining that the controversy was largely a misunderstanding.

"The humanity to which the Blessed Virgin Mary gave birth always was that of the Son of God himself. That is the reason why the Assyrian Church of the East is praying the Virgin Mary as "the Mother of Christ our God and Saviour." In the light of this same faith the Catholic tradition addresses the Virgin Mary as "the Mother of God" and also as "the Mother of Christ." We both recognize the legitimacy and rightness of these expressions of the same faith and we both respect the preference of each Church in her liturgical life and piety.

This is the unique faith that we profess in the mystery of Christ. The controversies of the past led to anathemas, bearing on persons and on formulas. The Lord's Spirit permits us to understand better today that the divisions brought about in this way were due in large part to misunderstandings." – *COMMON CHRISTOLOGICAL DECLARATION BETWEEN THE CATHOLIC CHURCH AND THE ASSYRIAN CHURCH OF THE EAST, Given* at Saint Peter's, on 11 November 1994, http://www.vatican.va/roman_curia/pontifical_councils/chrstuni/doc uments/rc_pc_chrstuni_doc_11111994_assyrian-church_en.html

[82] Ilaria L.E. Ramelli, *The Christian Doctrine of Apokatastasis,* BRILL, Leiden Boston, 2013, p. 11

[83] St. Augustine, *Enchiridion: On Faith, Hope and Love*, Chapter xxix, 112, translated by Albert C. Outler, 1955

[84] Cf. Edward Beecher, *History of Opinions on the Scriptural Doctrine of Retribution*, D. Appleton and Company, New York, 1878, p. 189ff

[85] Cf. Edward Beecher, *History of Opinions on the Scriptural Doctrine of Retribution*, D. Appleton and Company, New York, 1878, Universalism Asserted, p. 148, quoted by Hanson, p. 224

[86] J.W. Hanson, *Universalism: The Prevailing Doctrine of the Christian Church During Its First Five Hundred Years*, Universalist Publishing House, Boston and Chicago, 1899, p. 23
One example in contemporary literature demonstrates that the talismatic power of God as Father still resonates with Christians

today. *The Shack* by William Paul Young is a 2007 novel by a first-time author who depicted "Papa" as a loving God who never gives up on His children. Its success astounded the publishing world by selling over 25 million copies and becoming one of the top 70 best-selling books of all time. Although the book was initially attacked in America by some conservative evangelicals – and Young was called a heretic – *The Shack* has been published in 39 languages and made into a major motion picture.

Chapter 5 – What do the ancient creeds tell us?

[87] "Status of Global Mission, 2014, in the Context of AD 1800–2025" –

http://www.gordonconwell.edu/resources/documents/StatusOfGlobalMission.pdf

[88] Conc. Ephes. Can. VII. *"'The holy Synod has determined that no person shall be allowed to bring forward, or to write, or to compose any other Creed (ἑτέραν πίστιν μηδενὶ ἐξεῖναι προφέρειν ἤγουν συγγράφειν ἤ συντιθέναι), besides that which was settled by the holy fathers who assembled in the city of Nicæa, with the Holy Spirit. But those who shall dare to compose any other Creed, or to exhibit or produce any such, if they are bishops or clergymen, they shall be deposed, but if they are of the laity, they shall be anathematized.' The Council of Chalcedon (451), although setting forth a new definition of faith, repeated the same prohibition (after the Defin. Fidei)."* – Philip Schaff, *Creeds of Christendom, with a History and Critical notes*, Volume I, The History of Creeds, Harper & Brothers, 1877, p 35

[89] The Apostles Creed probably took its present form between AD 250 and 350. It is first found in Rufinus, who wrote at the end of the fourth and beginning of the fifth century. No allusion is made to it before this by Justin Martyr, Clement, Origen, the historian Eusebius or any of their contemporaries.

[90] Philip Schaff, *Creeds of Christendom, with a History and Critical notes*, Volume I, The History of Creeds, Harper & Brothers, 1877, p 14

[91] Philip Schaff, *Creeds of Christendom, with a History and Critical notes*, Volume I, The History of Creeds, Harper & Brothers, 1877, p 14. Words may vary in some contemporary versions of the Creed.

---

[92] or *ages* - αἰώνων in Greek

[93] In the late 6th century, the Latin-speaking Western Church added the words *"and the Son"* to the description of the procession of the Holy Spirit. The Eastern Church argued that this was a violation of Canon VII of the Third Ecumenical Council, since the words were not included in the text by either the Council of Nicea or that of Constantinople.

[94] Philip Schaff, *The Creeds of Christendom with a History and Critical Notes*, Vol. I, Harper & Brothers, 1877, Sixth Edition Revised and Enlarged, by David S. Schaff, 1905, 1919, p. 28-29. Words may vary in some contemporary versions of the Creed.
In the original creed as set forth at Nicea, there was added a condemnation against the Arians that was not included in the revised creed when it was finalized at the council at Constantinople. The Arians had taught that Jesus was a created being, and not God. The anathema read, *"But those who say, 'There was a time when he was not,"* and *"He was not before he was made,' and 'He was made out of nothing,' or 'He is of another substance' or 'essence,' or 'The Son of God is created,' or 'changeable,' or 'alterable' – they are condemned by the holy catholic and apostolic Church. "*

[95] The condemnatory statements read, *"Whosoever will be saved, before all things it is necessary that he hold the Catholic Faith. Which Faith except everyone do keep whole and undefiled, without doubt he shall perish everlastingly. . . . And they that have done good shall go into life everlasting, and they that have done evil into everlasting fire. This is the Catholic Faith, which except a man believe faithfully and firmly, he cannot be saved."* – Athanasian Creed, *New Advent*, http://www.newadvent.org/cathen/02033b.htm

[96] Philip Schaff, *The Creeds of Christendom with a History and Critical Notes*, Vol. I, Harper & Brothers, 1877, Sixth Edition Revised and Enlarged, by David S. Schaff, 1905, 1919, p. 38

Chapter 6 – What happened in the Middle Ages?

[97] Rob Bell, *Love Wins: A Book About Heaven, Hell, and the Fate of Every Person Who Ever Lived*, HarperOne, 2011

[98] April 14, 2011

[99] The ancient historian Polybius lived ca. 203-120 BC. He is

renowned for his ideas of political balance in government, and has been looked to throughout history by those interested in establishing republican forms of government – including the Founding Fathers who framed the U.S. Constitution. He wrote, *". . . as every multitude is fickle, full of lawless desires, unreasoned passion, and violent anger, the multitude must be held in by invisible terrors and suchlike pageantry. For this reason I think not that the ancients acted rashly and at haphazard in introducing among the people notions concerning the gods and beliefs in the terrors of hell, but that the moderns are most rash and foolish in banishing such beliefs."* – Polybius, *Histories*, Book VI, 56

Strabo (63/64 BC – ca. AD 24), an ancient historian, geographer and philosopher agreed. He was a proponent of Roman imperialism. He wrote, *"Most of those who live in the cities are incited to emulation by the myths that are pleasing . . . but they are deterred from evil courses when, either through descriptions or through typical representations of objects unseen, they learn of divine punishments, terrors, and threats . . . a philosopher cannot influence them by reason or exhort them to reverence, piety or faith; nay, there is need of religious fear also, and this cannot be aroused without myths and marvels. For thunderbolts, aegis, trident, torches, snakes, thyrsus-lances – arms of the gods – are myths, and so is the entire ancient theology. But the founders of states gave their sanction to these things . . . to scare the simple-minded."* – Strabo, *The Geography of Strabo 1.2.8*, The Loeb Classical Lilbrary, translated by Horace Leonard Jones, London: William Heinemann, New York: G. P. Putnam's & Sons, 1917, pp. 69

[100] This claim eventually developed into the official Roman Catholic teaching that, *"The Pope, Bishop of Rome and Peter's successor . . . by reason of his office as Vicar of Christ, and as pastor of the entire Church has full, supreme, and universal power over the whole Church, a power which he can always exercise unhindered. . . . The Pope enjoys, by divine institution, 'supreme, full, immediate, and universal power in the care of souls.'"* – *Catechism of the Catholic Church*, paragraph 882, Paragraph 937.

[101] Saint Robert Bellarmine, in his *Treatise on Civil Government*, discussed the history of this development in the church of the Middle Ages. Bellarmine (1542-1621) was one of the most important cardinals of the Catholic Reformation. His monumental work, *Disputationes*, systematized the various controversies facing

the Church and is still considered a classic today. He wrote: *"John Huss . . . asserted that it is not permitted to hand over an incorrigible heretic to the secular power and to allow the penalty of burning. Luther held the same . . . All Catholics teach the contrary, and even some of the heretics. For Calvin, after he had publicly punished as a heretic Michael Servetus with the ultimate penalty . . . published a book in which he demonstrates that it is permissible to take notice of heretics with a sword."* – St. Robert Bellarmine, *Treatise on Civil Government*, Chapter XXI

[102] The Roman Catholic Church and the Anglican Communion consider Augustine a saint and pre-eminent Doctor of the Church. Many Protestants, especially those of a Calvinist or Reformed persuasion, consider him to be one of the theological fathers of the Reformation teaching on salvation and divine grace. In the Eastern Orthodox Church he is called "Blessed Augustine," although a minority consider him a heretic because of the clause he added to the Nicene Creed saying that the Holy Spirit proceeds from the Father *"and the Son."*

[103] St. Augustine, *Confessions*, Book 1, Chapter 1

[104] St. Augustine, *Confessions*, Book 1, chapters 13 & 14

[105] Augustine *"mostly used what is termed the Vetus Latina, the "Old Latin" version of Biblical texts . . . The 'Old Latin' translations were of varying quality, depending on the Books of the Bible concerned, and presented many erroneous readings which the user was not always able to detect. In fact, Augustine in his Retractions admitted that several times he had made incorrect interpretations on the basis of false translations (Retr. 2,12,39)"* – http://www.augnet.org/?ipageid=1741

[106] St. Augustine, *City of God*, Book XXI, Chapter 3

[107] *"And had it been inflicted on all, no one could justly have found fault with the justice of Him who takes vengeance; whereas, in the deliverance of so many from that just award, there is cause to render the most cordial thanks to the gratuitous bounty of Him who delivers."* – St. Augustine, *City of God*, Book XXI, Chapter 3

[108] St. Augustine, *City of God*, Book XXI, Chapter 3, *A Select Library of Nicene and Post-Nicene Fathers,* edited by Philip Schaff, Vol. II, St. Augustin's: City of God and Christian Doctrine, T&T Clark,

223

Edinburgh, p. 453

[109] Augustine, *A Select Library of the Nicene and Post-Nicene Fathers of the Christian Church, The Writings Against the Manichaeans and Against the Donatists*, Volume IV, chapter 6, Philip Schaff, T&T Clark, Edinburgh, p. 641

Augustine ruled out the punishment of death because he judged that this was unbecoming the gentleness of the Church. There was also no imperial law in existence during his lifetime that would allow heretics to be sentenced to death. That Law, *"Quicumque, C. de hereticis,"* was promulgated shortly after Augustine died. – cf. St. Robert Bellarmine, *Treatise on Civil Government*, Chapter XXI

[110] As expressed by one critic, *". . . Albigensian crusades, Spanish armadas, Netherland's butcheries, St. Bartholomew massacres, the accursed infamies of the Inquisition, the vile espionage, the hideous bale fires of Seville and Smithfield, the racks, the gibbets, the thumbscrews, the subterranean torture chambers used by churchly torturers who assumed 'the garb and language of priests with the trade and temper of executioners,' to sicken, crush, and horrify the revolted conscience of mankind."* – Frederick W. Farrar, *Lives of the Fathers*, Vol. II, Adam and Charles Black, Edinburgh, 1889, p. 536

[111] Hans Urs von Balthasar, *Dare We Hope "That All Men Be Saved?"*, Ignatius Press, San Francisco, 1988, p. 64

[112] *". . . a transformation and renewal of the whole human race that is all-encompassing, natural, and by grace, from death and corruption to immortal life and incorruption in the expected resurrection."* – Maximus, *Expositio in Psalmum 59* (PG 91:857A). Quoted by Ian A. McFarland, Scottish Journal of Theology Ltd, SJT 58(4): 410–433 (2005)

[113] St. Isaac of Nineveh, *Isaac of Nineveh, The Second Part'*, *chapters IV-XLI*, translated by Sebastian Brock, Corpus Scriptorum Christianorum Orientalium 555, Scriptores syri 225, Louvain, 1995, 39:6, 15-16, quoted by Bishop Hilarion Alfeyev in a *paper delivered at the World Congress on Divine Mercy, Lateran Basilica, Rome, 4 April 2008*

[114] Richard Eddy, *Universalism in America*, Volume I, Universalist Publishing House, Boston, 1884, pp. 7- 8

[115] *"Apocatastasis,"* *New Schaff-Herzog Encyclopedia of Religious Knowledge*, Vol. I, Baker Book House, Grand Rapids, MI, 1951

Chapter 7 – What happened from then to now?

[116] Edward Beecher, *History of Opinions on the Scriptural Doctrine of Retribution*, D. Appleton and Company, New York, 1878

[117] www.tentmaker.org

[118] www.tentmaker.org – home page

[119] Quoted by F.W. Farrar, from Luther's Briefe, ii. 454, *Mercy and Judgment*, MacMillan and Company, London, 1881, p. 24

[120] http://bookofconcord.org/augsburgconfession.php

[121] ChristianUniversalist.org The History of Universalism

[122] Richard Eddy, *Universalism in America*, Volume I, Universalist Publishing House, Boston, 1884, p. 10

Article 42 said, *"All men shall not be saved at the length. They also are worthy of condemnation, who endeavor, at this time, to restore the dangerous opinion, that all men, be they never so ungodly, shall at length be saved, when they have suffered pains for their sins a certain time appointed by God's justice."* – Article 42 – Legh Richmond, *A selection from the writings of the reformers and early Protestant divines of the Church of England*, Volume 2, published by John Hatchard, Bookseller to the Queen, London, 1817, p. 338

[123] William Law, *An Humble, Affectionate, and Earnest Address to the Clergy*, typed in electronic format by William White, from the 1974 Georg Olms Verlag (Hildesheim New York) edition of *The Works of the Reverend William Law*, [Addr-191, 192] , http://www.ccel.org/ccel/law/clergy.i.html

[124] Andrew Jukes, *The Second Death and the Restitution of All Things*, Concordant Publishing Concern, reprint 2001, Santa Clarita, CA, pp. 27-28

[125] Andrew Jukes, *The Second Death and the Restitution of All Things*, Concordant Publishing Concern, reprint 2001, Santa Clarita, CA, pp. 117-118

[126] C. S. Lewis, *George MacDonald: An Anthology*, The MacMillan Company, New York, 1947, pp. 18-20
It should be noted that C. S. Lewis did *not* hold to a belief in restoration. He was, nonetheless, deeply influenced by MacDonald.
[127] George MacDonald, *Unspoken Sermons*, Third Series, "Justice"

[128] F. W. Farrar, *Mercy and Judgment*, MacMillan and Company, London, 1881, p. 485

[129] George T. Knight, "Universalists," *New Schaff-Herzog Encyclopedia of Religious Knowledge*, Funk & Wagnalls, London, 1909, Vol. 12, p. 96

[130] In the Preface of the book, he explains his basic premise and how he came to his conclusions. *"The whole human race are considered in the following work, as made for happiness; and it finally fixes them in the everlasting enjoyment of it . . . What I therefore now offer to the world is not the result of my own imagination, or wisdom: Nor was it fetched from any scheme of man's invention; but solely from the fountain of revealed truth, the inspired oracles of God. These were my governing rule in this enquiry; and I have taken great care, and spared no pains, that I might understand them in their genuine sense."* – Charles Chauncy, *The Mystery hid from Ages and Generations, made manifest by the Gospel-Revelation, or, The Salvation of All Men*, London, 1784, reprinted by Applewood Books, Bedford, MA, pp. v-vi

[131] Charles Chauncy, *The Mystery hid from Ages and Generations, made manifest by the Gospel-Revelation, or, The Salvation of All Men*, London, 1784, reprinted by Applewood Books, Bedford, MA, pp.1-2

[132] Thomas Fessenden, *A Theoretic Explanation of the Science of Sanctity*, printed by William Fessenden, Brattleboro, 1804, p. 166

[133] He went on to say, *"My conviction of the truth of this doctrine was derived from reading the works of Stonehouse, Seigvolk, White, Chauncey and Winchester, and afterwards from an attentive perusal of the Scriptures. I always admitted with each of those authors future punishment, and of long duration."* – Benjamin Rush, *A Memorial containing Travels Through Life or Sundry Incidents in the Life of Dr. Benjamin Rush*, written by himself, published privately for the benefit of his descendants by Louis Alexander Biddle, Philadelphia, 1905, p. 125

[134] ChristianUniversalist.org The History of Universalism

[135] Elhanan Winchester, *The Universal Restoration Exhibited in Four Dialogues Between a Minister and His Friend*, Bill Blake & Company, Bellows Falls, VT, 1819, pp. 218, 219.

[136] Edward Beecher, *History of Opinions on the Scriptural Doctrine of Retribution*, D. Appleton and Company, New York, 1878, p. 297

[137] J.W. Hanson, *The Bible Hell*, Published at the Office of "The New Covenant," Chicago, 1878, p. 1

[138] At the end of the nineteenth century, it held state conventions or their equivalent in 42 states, supported four colleges, including Tufts College, later to become Tufts University which it founded in 1852, three theological schools and four finishing schools or academies. – George T. Knight, "Universalists," *New Schaff-Herzog Encyclopedia of Religious Knowledge*, Funk & Wagnalls, London, 1909, Vol. 12, p. 97

[139] It began as a diverse group of German Anabaptists, Moravians, Quakers, and people influenced by the Pietist movements, such as Methodism. In 1790, they held a convention in Philadelphia to discuss issues of polity and draw up a profession of faith. These Articles of Faith show their original orientation.

Of the Holy Scriptures. We believe the Scriptures of the Old and New Testament to contain a revelation of the perfections and will of God, and the rule of faith and practice.

Of the Supreme Being. We believe in one God, infinite in all his perfections, and that these perfections are all modifications of infinite, adorable, incomprehensible, and unchangeable love.

Of the Mediator. We believe that there is one Mediator between God and men, the man Christ Jesus, in whom dwelleth all the fullness of the Godhead bodily, who, by giving himself a ransom for all, hath redeemed them to God by his blood; and who, by the merit of his death, and the efficacy of his spirit, will finally restore the whole human race to happiness.

Of the Holy Ghost. We believe in the Holy Ghost, whose office is to make known to sinners the truth of their salvation, through the medium of the Holy Scriptures, and to reconcile the hearts of the children of men to God, and thereby to dispose them to genuine holiness.

Of Good Works. We believe in the obligation of the moral law, as to the rule of life; and we hold that the love of God manifested to man in a Redeemer, is the best means of producing obedience to that law, and promoting a holy, active and useful life. – Cf. Richard

Eddy, *Universalism in America – A History Vol. I*, Universalist Publishing House, Boston, 1884, pp. 297-298

[140] G. T. Flanders D.D, "Article XXXII, The Bible," *The Universalist Quarterly and General Review*, New Series, Volume XX, Universalist Publishing House, Boston, 1883, p. 464

[141] ChristianUniversalist.org The History of Universalism – http://www.christianuniversalist.org/resources/articles/history-of-universalism/

[142] http://www.uua.org/visitors/index.shtml

[143] Andreas Andreopoulos, "Eschatology and final restoration (apokatastasis) in Origen, Gregory of Nyssa and Maximos the Confessor," *Theandros, An Online Journal of Orthodox Christian Theology and Philosophy*, Volume 1, Number 3, Spring 2004 (changed slightly by the request of the author)

[144] Avery Cardinal Dulles, S.J., "The Population of Hell," *First Things*, May, 2003.

The *Catechism* was commissioned by the Synod of Bishops at the request of Pope John Paul II in 1985, entrusted to a commission of twelve Cardinals and Bishops chaired by then Cardinal Joseph Ratzinger a year later, and first approved by Pope John Paul II in June of 1991.

[145] Hans Urs von Balthasar, *Dare We Hope "That All Men Be Saved"?*, Ignatius Press, San Francisco, 1988, p. 16

[146] Cf. "Why so many people – including scientists – suddenly believe in an afterlife," by Brian Bethune, *Maclean's*, Tuesday, May 7, 2013 – http://www2.macleans.ca/2013/05/07/the-heaven-boom/

[147] Cf. Robert M. Bowman, Jr., PhD, Executive Director, Institute for Religious Research, copyright 2003, 2015, RW Research, Inc., Rose Publishing, Inc. See also http://www.ucc.org/beliefs_statement-of-faith

[148] *"We recognise that the interpretation of hell as eternal conscious punishment is the one most widely attested by the Church in its historic formulation of doctrine and in its understanding of Scripture. We also recognise that it represents the classic, mainstream evangelical position."* – David Hilborn (ed.) "The Nature of Hell, A Report by the Evangelical Alliance Commission on Unity and Truth

among Evangelicals (ACUTE)," Carlisle: Paternoster Press 2000, pp. 130-135

[149] http://www.sbc.net/bfm2000/bfm2000.asp

[150] Chapter III, Article III, Of God's Eternal Decree.

[151] "Statement of Faith," National Association of Evangelicals, http://nae.net/statement-of-faith/

[152] https://billygraham.org/about/what-we-believe/

[153] Cf. John Wenham, John Stott, Clark Pinnock and others

[154] Their influence can be seen in another statement in the ACUTE report mentioned above, *"Evangelicals diverge on whether hell is eternal in duration or effect – that is, whether an individual's punishment in hell will literally go on 'for ever', as a ceaseless conscious experience, or whether it will end in a destruction which will be 'forever', in the sense of being final and irreversible. It should be acknowledged that both of these interpretations preserve the crucial principle that judgment is on the basis of sins committed in this life, and that when judgment is to hell, it cannot be repealed (Matt. 25:41-6; Mark. 9:43-8; Luke 16:26)."*

[155] Cf. Jan Bonda, *The One Purpose of God: An Answer to the Doctrine of Endless Punishment*, William. B. Eerdmans Publishing Company, 1998
Thomas Talbott, *The Inescapable Love of God*, Universal Publishers/uPUBLISH.com, 1999, revised printing 9/2002
Gregory MacDonald (pseudonym), *The Evangelical Universalist*, Cascade Books, 2006 (in the Fall of 2009 Robin Parry acknowledged that he is the author)
Gerry Beauchmin, *Hope Beyond Hell*, Malista Press, newly revised 2010
Ilaria L.E. Ramelli, *The Christian Doctrine of Apokatastasis,* BRILL, Leiden Boston, 2013

An extensive internet site addressing the issue from an evangelical perspective is www.tentmaker.org, maintained by Gary and Michelle Amirault

[156] Thomas Talbott, *Universal Salvation: The Current Debate*, edited by Robin A. Parry and Christopher H. Partridge, Wm. B. Eerdmans, 2004, pp. 5-6. Talbott went on to ask, *"Why, after all, should an assumption concerning everlasting punishment be the only*

unquestioned assumption in a context where some are limiting the extent of God's love and others are limiting the scope of his ultimate victory? Why not at least examine the pros and cons of universal reconciliation alongside those of limited election and those of a limited victory over sin and death?. . . For even as many Augustinians are utterly convinced that God's salvific will cannot be defeated forever and many Arminians are utterly convinced that God at least wills the salvation of all human sinners, so I am equally convinced that both claims are true."

[157] The conference was attended by scholars, pastors and laypeople from the US, Canada and the UK specifically to discuss the three views of what happens to sinners after we die. cf. George W. Sarris, "Rethinking Hell Conference Challenges Beliefs," *ChristianPost.com*, July 1, 2015
– http://georgesarris.blogspot.com/2015/07/rethinking-hell-conference-challenges.html

[158] Jerry Walls, Professor of Philosophy and Scholar-in-Residence at Houston Baptist University

Chapter 8 – What does the Bible really say?
Sheol & Hades

[159] Oxford Dictionaries online

[160] F.W. Farrar, *Mercy and Judgment*, MacMillan and Company, London, 1881, p. 371

[161] Joachim Jeremias, "αδησ", *Theological Dictionary of the New Testament*, Vol. I., William B. Eerdmans Publishing Company, Grand Rapids, MI, 1972, p. 147. cf. also Beecher, p. 12; 36; William L. Holladay, *A Concise Hebrew and Aramaic Lexicon of the Old Testament*, William B. Eerdmans Publishing Company, Grand Rapids, MI, 1971, p. 356; Brown, Driver, Briggs, *A Hebrew and English Lexicon of the Old Testament*, pp. 982,983

[162] Joachim Jeremias, "αδησ" *Theological Dictionary of the New Testament*, Vol. I., William B. Eerdmans Publishing Company, Grand Rapids, MI, 1972, pp. 146,147

[163] William Shedd, *The Doctrine of Endless Punishment*, New York, Charles Scribner's Sons, 1886, p. 29

---

[164] Genesis 37:35

[165] 1 Samuel 2:6

[166] Numbers 16:32-33

[167] Jonah 2:2

[168] The Greek text used by the translators of the KJV has "*Hades*" in I Corinthians 15:55, where it translates it as "grave." The NIV and other modern translations follow a different manuscript version that considers "death" to be the correct word in this verse, not *Hades*. In the UBS Greek New Testament, "*Hades*" is listed as the last suggestion by the editors, who give the reading with "death" a B rating.

[169] The 2011 revision of the NIV has corrected the text to now read, *"In Hades, where he was in torment . . ."*

[170] Matthew 11:23 and Luke 10:15 NIV
The term is used in these verses in a manner similar to Isaiah 14:9, 11, and 15 where Babylon is said to be brought down to *Sheol* (*Hades* in the Septuagint, the Greek translation of the Old Testament), to denote debasement and overthrow. It is there translated "grave" in the NIV. *"The grave (sheol/hades) below is all astir to meet you at your coming.... All your pomp has been brought down to the grave (sheol/hades). . . But you are brought down to the grave (sheol/hades), to the depths of the pit."*

[171] Revelation 1:18

[172] Other references in the book of Revelation again have death and *Hades* linked together. In Revelation 6:8, John says, *"I looked, and there before me was a pale horse! Its rider was named Death, and Hades was following close behind him. They were given power over a fourth of the earth to kill by sword, famine and plague, and by the wild beasts of the earth."* The passage has nothing to do with torments in the future world. It talks of Death and *Hades* having destructive power in this world – they were given power to kill by sword, famine, plague, and wild beasts on *earth*.

[173] Cf. H. Bietenhard, Hell, *hades*, *The New International Dictionary of New Testament Theology*, Vol. 2, Zondervan Publishing House, Grand Rapids, MI, 1976, fifth printing October 1979, p.207

[174] Revelation 20:13

175 Luke 16:19-31

176 The parable occurs as the last in a series of five parables – The Lost Sheep, The Lost Coin, The Prodigal Son, The Unjust Steward, and The Rich Man and Lazarus. It begins with words that are exactly the same or very similar to the words at the beginning of two of the other parables. The Rich Man and Lazarus starts with, "There was a rich man..." The parable of the Unjust Steward begins in exactly the same way, "There was a rich man..." The parable of The Prodigal Son commences with a similar comment, "There was a man..."

177 What He did was similar to what a modern speaker would do when making reference to a book like *The Lion, the Witch and the Wardrobe* from the *Chronicles of Narnia*. He could clearly point out some very important truths about life in this world, without putting his stamp of approval on the existence of talking animals in another world.

178 The first part is derived from well-known folk material relating to the reversal of fortune in the afterlife. – Kacy Madsen , "The Rich Man & Lazarus," quoting Jeremias, http://wesley.nnu.edu/fileadmin/imported_site/biblical_studies/parabl es/ma-lk16_19-31.htm.

It was originally an Egyptian folktale of the journey of Si-Osiris, the son of Setme Chamois, to the underworld. That story concludes with these words: *He who has been good on earth, will be blessed in the kingdom of the dead, and he who has been evil on earth, will suffer in the kingdom of the dead.* The story was later brought into Palestine by Alexandrian Jews, where it became popular as the story of the poor scholar and a rich tax collector named Bar Ma'jan.

179 Years later, in AD 70, the Roman legions came and destroyed the city of Jerusalem and the Temple, even as Jesus had elsewhere predicted. The religious leaders were deposed from their high positions and experienced great suffering at the hands of the Roman legions. But even then, they did not believe that He was their promised Messiah. They hardened their hearts even after One had been raised from the dead.

180 Isaiah referred to that future time when, *"Every valley shall be raised up, every mountain and hill made low; the rough ground shall become level, the rugged places a plain. And the glory of the LORD will be revealed, and all mankind will see it. For the mouth of the*

LORD has spoken." – Isaiah 40:4-5

Chapter 9 – What does the Bible really say?
Gehenna & Tartarus

[181] Jesus uses the word in Matthew 5:22, 29 & 30, Matthew 10:28, Matthew 18:9; Matthew 23:15 & 33, Mark 9:43, 45 & 47; and in Luke 12:5. The other use is James 3:6.

[182] *"Ge Hinnom"* It's also called *"Gai ben-Hinnom,"* meaning "Valley of the son of Hinnom." It's the name given to the Wadi er-rabibi in South Jerusalem located outside the south wall of the ancient city and stretching from the foot of present Mount Zion eastward to the Kidron Valley.

[183] It's first mentioned as part of the descriptions of the land allotted to the tribes of Judah and Benjamin in Joshua 15:8 and 18:16. In Nehemiah 11:30, it's mentioned as a description of where the people of Judah lived.

[184] "Tophet," Easton's Illustrated Dictionary

[185] II Kings 23:10

[186] Jeremiah 7:32-33; 19:6-9

[187] F. W. Farrar, *Eternal Hope*, Preface to First Edition, 1892 – Five Sermons Preached in Westminster Abbey November and December 1877

[188] Ecclesiastes 6:3

[189] H. Bietenhard, Hell, *geenna*, *The New International Dictionary of New Testament Theology*, Vol. 2, Zondervan Publishing House, Grand Rapids, MI, 1976, fifth printing October 1979, p. 208

[190] The first Christian uses of *Gehenna* in the modern sense of a place of torment after death are by Justin Martyr and Clement of Alexandria about AD 150-195. Since Clement was actually a believer in ultimate restoration, it is clear that the word did not then carry with it the meaning of endless punishment – cf. J.W. Hanson, *The Bible Hell*, published at the office of "The New Covenant," Chicago, 1878, pp. 47- 48

[191] Origen, *Against Celsus*, Book VI, Chapter XXV

[192] The Targum of Jonathan ben Uzziel. See Geza Vermes, *Scripture and Tradition in Judaism*, 1973, p. 3; J.W. Hanson, *The Bible Hell*, p. 47

[193] F.W. Farrar, *Mercy and Judgment*, MacMillan and Company, London, 1881, p. 199

[194] Simcha Paull Raphael. *Jewish Views of the Afterlife*, Jason Aronson, Inc., Northvale, NJ, 1994, pp. 144-145.

F.W. Farrar lists numerous Talmudic and Jewish authorities to support this conclusion that *Gehenna* was not normally understood by the Jews to mean what is generally inferred by the modern term *hell*. The following are just a few:
Gibborim, f. 70, I, Nishmath Chajim, p. 83, I, Jalkuth Shimeoni, f. 83, 3, &c., all say that twelve months is the period of punishment in Gehenna.
Emek Hammelech, f. 138, 4: *"The wicked stay in Gehenna till the Resurrection, and then the Messiah, passing through it, redeems them."* The same treatise (f. 16, 2), says even of the worst sinners, like those of Sodom, and spies who betray Jews, that they are punished *"till the time decreed is expired,"* and then allowed to transmigrate.
Midrash Rabba, I, 30. Avoda Zara, 3. *"After the last judgment Gehenna exists no longer."*
Asarah Maamaroth, f. 85, I: *"There will hereafter be no Gehenna."*
Jalkuth Shimeoni, f. 46, I: Gabriel and Michael will open the 8,000 gates of Gehenna and let out Israelites and righteous Gentiles.
Jalkuth Chadash, f. 57, I: *"The righteous bring out of Gehenna imperfect souls."*
Jalkuth Koheleth: *"God created Paradise and Gehenna, that those in the one should deliver those in the other."*
Rabbi Bar Nachman: *"The future world (the Olam habba) will have its Gehenna, but the last times will have it no more."*
Joreh Deah ad fin.: *"As is commonly said, 'The punishment of wicked Israelites in Gehenna is twelve months.'"*
Rabbi Akiba, the second Moses, the second Ezra. *"The duration of the punishment of the wicked in Gehenna is twelve months."* Edyoth, ii. 10
F.W. Farrar, *Mercy and Judgment*, MacMillan and Company, London, 1881, pp. 203ff.

[195] Mt. 5:21-22

---

[196] W.E. Vine, "Fool," *Expository Dictionary of New Testament Words*, Vol. II, Fleming H. Revell Company, 1940, seventeenth impression, 1966, p. 114

[197] Matthew 5:28-30. Jesus makes similar statements in Matthew 18:8-9 and Mark 9:43-48 where one's foot is added to the list of bodily members to be cut off in order not to sin.

[198] Mark 9:43-48

[199] Eusebius, *Ecclesiastical History of Eusebius Pamphilus*, Book VI, chapter 41, translated by Christian Frederick Cruse, Stanford & Swords, New York, 1850, p. 259, see translator's note, pp. 259-260. He was referring to Julian, Cronion, Epimachus, and Alexander.

The ancient Greek writer Strabo described the sacred precinct of Athena in the city of Athens. He said it comprised *"both the temple of Athena Polias, in which is the lamp that is never quenched, and the Parthenon built by Ictinus."* The fire he referred to was later extinguished – Strabo, *Geography*, Book IX, chapter 1, paragraph 16, published in volume IV of the Loeb Classical Library edition, 1927

[200] Flavius Josephus, *The War of the Jews*, Book II, chapter 17, paragraph 6

[201] Matthew 5:26

[202] Matthew 10:28, Luke 12:5

[203] *Psuche*

[204] Matthew 10:39
[205] Matthew 10:29-31; cf. Luke 12:6-7

[206] Matthew 23:15

[207] Matthew 23:33

[208] James 3:6

[209] II Peter 2:4, English Standard Version

[210] The apocryphal book of Enoch

Chapter 10 – How long is *forever* anyway? *Aion, Olam & Kolasis*

[211] Beecher, p. 141. Cf. also Sasse, "αιων", *Theological Dictionary of the New Testament*, Vol. I, pp. 198ff

Various definitions have been given through the centuries. Theodoret, writing between AD 300 and 400, wrote, *"Aion is not any existing thing, but an interval denoting time, sometimes infinite when spoken of God, sometimes proportioned to the duration of the creation, and sometimes to the life of man."* Hesychius (AD 400-600) defines it as *"The life of man, the time of life."* John of Damascus (AD 750) says, *"The life of every man is called aion. . . . The whole duration of life of this world is called aion. The life after the resurrection is called 'the aion to come.'"* In the sixteenth century, Phavorinus added the concept of endless, but added that it was placed there because that was the understanding of the theologians. *"Aion, time, also life, also habit, or way of life. Aion is also the eternal and endless as it seems to the Theologian."* – cf. J.W. Hanson, *Aion, Aionios*, Published by the Author, Third Edition, Chicago, 1878, p. 12

The Dictionary of New Testament Theology explains that *". . . one can only consider the designation of 'antiquity' or the 'far future' as the essential NT use of the word."* – J. Guhrt, Time, *aion*, *The New International Dictionary of New Testament Theology*, Vol. 3, Zondervan Publishing House, Grand Rapids, MI, 1971, 1978, fourth printing October 1979, p. 829

[212] In the nineteenth century, German scholar Johann Schleusner wrote an extensive lexicon of both the Septuagint and the New Testament. He defined *aion* as *"Any space of time, whether longer or shorter, past, present or future, to be determined by the persons or things spoken of, and the scope of the subjects; the life or age of man; Aionios, a definite and long period of time, that is, a long continued, but still definite period of time."* – *The Universalist Quarterly and General Review*, Volume IV, A. Thompkins, Boston, 1847, pp. 19-20.

[213] *Aion* is used frequently in the Greek classics, but never in the sense of eternity. As a noun, it occurs 13 times in *The Iliad* and *The Odyssey*, but Homer *never* uses it to signify eternal duration. It is

used to signify human existence, the state of being alive among men. For example, in the *Iliad*, Priam, endeavoring to persuade Hector to enter the city and avoid the encounter with Achilles, says, "*Thyself shall be deprived of pleasant aionos* (life or existence)." - *Iliad*, xxii.58, *autos de filas aionos amerthas, The Iliad of Homer, according to the text of Wolf*, John J. Owen, D. Appleton & Co., New York, 1867, p. 425
Later, when Andromache laments over the dead body of Hector, she says, "*Husband, thou hast perished from aionos* (life or existence)."– *Iliad*, xxiv.725, *aner, ap' aionos neos oleo, The Iliad of Homer, according to the text of Wolf*, John J. Owen, D. Appleton & Co., New York, 1867, p. 486

[214] In all but four times in the Old Testament, *aion* is the Greek translation of the Hebrew *olam*. The noun form occurs 394 times, and the adjective 110 times. In Exodus it refers twelve times out of fourteen to things that have passed away; in Leviticus twenty-four times, always of things that have come to an end; in Numbers ten times; in Deuteronomy ten times out of twelve; and so on throughout the Old Testament. – F.W. Farrar, *Mercy and Judgment*, MacMillan and Company, London, 1881, p. 378

[215] Exodus 21:6, English Standard Version

[216] Cf. New International Version, Revised Standard Version, New Revised Standard Version, New Living Translation, Good News Translation, The Message

[217] For example, in Leviticus 6:18 we're told, "*All the males among the children of Aaron shall eat of it. It shall be a statute for ever in your generations concerning the offerings of the LORD made by fire.*" The NIV communicates the correct sense with, "*Any male descendant of Aaron may eat it. It is his regular share of the offerings made to the LORD by fire for the generations to come.*" See also Leviticus 7:36 and Numbers 10:8
[218] F.W. Farrar, *Mercy and Judgment*, MacMillan and Company, London, 1881, p. 379

[219] Genesis 49:26 – "*The blessings of your father are mighty beyond the blessings of my parents, up to the bounties of the everlasting hills.*"
Deuteronomy 33:15– "*. . . with the finest produce of the ancient mountains and the abundance of the everlasting hills*"
English Standard Version

---

[220] Isaiah 54:10 New King James Version

[221] Jonah 2:6

[222] *"I have consecrated this temple, which you have built, by putting my Name there forever."* – I Kings 9:3

[223] II Kings 25:8-9

[224] Revised Standard Version

[225] Psalm 148:4-6.
Forever and ever is the translation of *ad and olam* in Hebrew

[226] Revelation 21:1

[227] *"Your throne was established long ago; you are from all eternity."*
– Psalm 93:2
"For the LORD is good and his love endures forever; his faithfulness continues through all generations." – Psalm 100:5
"Praise the LORD, all you nations; extol him, all you peoples. For great is his love toward us, and the faithfulness of the LORD endures forever. Praise the LORD." – Psalm 117
"Give thanks to the LORD, for he is good; his love endures forever. Let Israel say: 'His love endures forever.' Let the house of Aaron say: 'His love endures forever.' Let those who fear the LORD say: 'His love endures forever.'" – Psalm 118:1-4

[228] *"It always means a period of time. Otherwise it would be impossible to account for the plural, or for such qualifying expressions as this age, or the age to come. It does not mean something endless or everlasting. . . . The adjective . . . means enduring through or pertaining to a period of time."* – Marvin R. Vincent, *Word Studies in the New Testament,* Vol. IV, Kessinger Publishing, 2004, p. 59

[229] Luke 1:33

[230] *"Then the end will come, when he hands over the kingdom to God the Father after he has destroyed all dominion, authority and power. For he must reign until he has put all his enemies under his feet. The last enemy to be destroyed is death. . . . When he has done this, then the Son himself will be made subject to him who put everything under him, so that God may be all in all."* – I Corinthians 15:24-28

[231] Young's Literal Translation

[232] *"Yet among the mature we do impart wisdom, although it is not a wisdom of this age or of the rulers of this age, who are doomed to pass away. But we impart a secret and hidden wisdom of God, which God decreed before the ages for our glorification. None of the rulers of this age understood this; for if they had, they would not have crucified the Lord of glory."* – I Corinthians 2:6-8, Revised Standard Version

[233] *"Now these things happened to them as a warning, but they were written down for our instruction, upon whom the end of the ages has come."* – I Corinthians 10:11

[234] *". . . so that in the ages to come he might show the immeasurable riches of his grace in kindness toward us in Christ Jesus."* – Ephesians 2:7, New Revised Standard Version

[235] Colossians 1:26

[236] *"In the New Testament the history of the world is conceived as developed through a succession of [ages]. A series of such [ages] precedes the introduction of a new series inaugurated by the Christian dispensation, and the end of the world and the second coming of Christ are to mark the beginning of another series. . . . The plural is also used, [ages] of the [ages], signifying all the successive periods which make up the sum total of the ages collectively. Rom. 16:27; Gal. 1:5; Philip. 4:20, etc. This plural phrase is applied by Paul to God only."* – Marvin R. Vincent, *Word Studies in the New Testament*, Vol. IV, Kessinger Publishing, 2004, p. 59

[237] For an exposition of this entire text from a restorationist perspective, see "Explanation of Matthew xxv, 46," *Universalist Quarterly and General Review*, Volume XX – No. 1, Thompkins & Co., Boston, January 1863, pp. 42-66

[238] St. Augustine, *City of God Against the Pagans*, tr. Henry Bettenson, (London:Penguin, 1972), 1001-2

[239] Thomas Scott, *A Commentary on the Holy Bible, Matthew*, Philadelphia, William S. Martien, No. 144 Chestnut Street, 1852, p. 192, emphasis in the original

[240] Robert W. Yarbrough, *Hell Under Fire*, general editors Christopher W. Morgan, Robert A Peterson, Zondervan 2004, p. 76,

quoting Moses Stuart, *Exegetical Essays on Several Words Relating to Future Punishment*, Philadelphia, Presbyterian Publishing Committee, 1867 [reprint of 1830 edition], p. 62, emphasis in the original

[241] Cf. Taylor Lewis, *Commentary on the Holy Scriptures, Ecclesiastes*, by John Peter Lange, Grand Rapids, Zondervan, p. 48. Although Lewis himself held to a belief in Endless Punishment, he stated very clearly that people who confront believers in ultimate restoration would commit an error and fail in their arguments if they focused on the significance of the words *aion* and *aionios* in an attempt to prove that they necessarily carry the meaning of endless duration. This also applies to Daniel's words in Daniel 12:2 – *"Multitudes who sleep in the dust of the earth will awake: some to everlasting life, others to shame and everlasting contempt."*

[242] The statements made in the Apostles' Creed and the Nicene Creed support this conclusion. The closing article of the Apostles' Creed is, *"I believe in the resurrection of the body, and the life everlasting."* However, the Nicene Creed has replaced the phrase with one explicitly stating *"the life of the world (age) to come."* If the word *aionios* in the Apostles' Creed was universally understood to mean endless at that time, it is highly improbable that the idea of endlessness would be later dropped, and a different concept put in its place. But if *life everlasting (zoein aionion)* was understood to mean the life of the world or age to come, then the Nicene Creed did not drop the idea at all.

[243] Josephus, writing in Greek, used the word *aion* to refer to the imprisonment of John the Tyrant by the Romans, the reputation of Herod, the rebuilt Temple which had already been destroyed when he wrote, and the worship in the Temple which was no longer being offered. In each of these cases, he applies the word to something that ended. As mentioned earlier, when referring to endless punishment, Josephus used terms that were unequivocal in their meaning, such as *aidion, athanaton,* and *adialeipton* – eternal, deathless, and never-ceasing.

Similarly, Philo generally used *aidion* to denote endless, and always used *aionion* to describe temporary duration. In one passage, he used the same phrase that Jesus used in Matthew 25:46 to refer to punishment. Philo states, *"It is better not to promise than not to give prompt assistance, for no blame follows in the former case, but in the latter there is dissatisfaction from the weaker class, and a deep hatred and everlasting punishment (kolasis aionios) from such as are more powerful."* Since the "more powerful" that Philo refers to are human rulers who can only inflict temporal punishments on the "weaker class," the context here makes it very clear that the punishment referred to is of this world. – cf. J.W. Hanson, *Aion, Aionios*, Jansen, McClurg & Co., Chicago, 1880, p.89, quoting from Fragments, Tom. II, p. 667, ed. Mangey, 1741

It is also worth noting that Origen, who believed that all creation would ultimately be restored, actually used the word *aionios* on some occasions to describe the punishment of the wicked. The Emperor Justinian, in his argument against Origen, did *not* use *aionios* to describe Origen's belief in the future endless punishment of the wicked. Justinian used the word, *ateleutetos*, which does mean "endless." – cf. Edward Beecher, *History of Opinions on the Spiritual Doctrine of Retribution*, D. Appleton and Company, New York, 1878, pp. 164,165

[244] This discourse extends without a break from Matthew 24:4 all the way to the actual passage in question, Matthew 25:46.

[245] William Barclay, *A Spiritual Autobiography*, William B. Eerdmans Publishing Company, Grand Rapids, 1977, pp. 65-67

[246] Some of the inscriptions that relate directly to our subject come from Phrygian and Lydian monuments of the imperial period. *"In these inscriptions the sins punished by deity are those against the deity itself . . . The deity smites the offender with sickness and infirmity, or even punishes himself or his family with death. The sinner can win back the grace of the deity only by open confession of his guilt. In this way alone can he be liberated from sickness and misfortune."* – Johannes Schneider, *"kolazo, kolasis,"* *Theological Dictionary of the New Testament*, Volume III, Wm. B. Eerdmans Publishing Company, Grand Rapids, MI, 1965, seventh printing, August 1977, pp. 814, 815

[247] Plato, *Protagoras*, translated by Benjamin Jowett

[248] W.E. Vine, "Punish," *An Expository Dictionary of New Testament Words*, Vol. III, Fleming H. Revell Company, Old Tappan, NJ, 1940, seventeenth impression, 1966, p. 230

[249] Johannes Schneider, *"kolazo, kolasis,"* *Theological Dictionary of the New Testament*, Volume III, Wm. B. Eerdmans Publishing

Company, Grand Rapids, MI, 1965, seventh printing, August 1977, p. 814.

[250] II Thessalonians 1:6 – *". . . since indeed God considers it just to repay with affliction those who afflict you"* – English Standard Version

[251] *Olethron* in Greek

[252] Luke 20:35-36

[253] John 10:27-29

[254] John 11:25-26 – *"I am the resurrection and the life. He who believes in me will live, even though he dies; and whoever lives and believes in me will never die (ou me apothane)."*

[255] Romans 8:38-39

[256] *"So will it be with the resurrection of the dead. The body that is sown is perishable, it is raised imperishable (aphtharsia) . . ."*
[257] *"For the perishable must clothe itself with the imperishable (aphtharsian), and the mortal with immortality (athanasian)."* – I Corinthians 15:53

[258] *"For as in Adam all die, so in Christ all will be made alive (zoopoiethesontai). –* I Corinthians 15:22

[259] *"Praise be to the God and Father of our Lord Jesus Christ! In his great mercy he has given us new birth into a living hope through the resurrection of Jesus Christ from the dead, and into an inheritance that can never perish (aphtharton), spoil (amianton) or fade (amaranton) . . . "* – I Peter 1:3 & 4

[260] *amarantinos* – I Peter 5:4

[261] J. Guhrt, Time, *aion, The New International Dictionary of New Testament Theology*, Vol. 3, Zondervan Publishing House, Grand Rapids, MI, 1971, 1978, fourth printing October 1979, p.832

[262] John 5:24

[263] When God is referred to as the *"eternal God"* in Romans 16:26, the proper translation is, *"the God of the ages."*

[264] Marvin R. Vincent, *Word Studies in the New Testament*, Vol. IV, Kessinger Publishing, 2004, p. 60

Chapter 11 – What are God's judgments all about?

[265] James 2:13

[266] Genesis 18:25

[267] *"If anyone takes the life of a human being, he must be put to death. Anyone who takes the life of someone's animal must make restitution – life for life. If anyone injures his neighbor, whatever he has done must be done to him: fracture for fracture, eye for eye, tooth for tooth."* – Leviticus 24:17-20

[268] *"Jesus said, "Father, forgive them, for they do not know what they are doing."* – Luke 23:34

[269] Leviticus 24:15-16

[270] The Apostle Paul made that very clear in Colossians 2:13-14 when he said that God *"forgave us all our sins."* And in I John 2:2, John told his readers just how far the impact of Christ's death on the cross extended. *"He is the atoning sacrifice for our sins, and not only for ours but also for the sins of the whole world."*

[271] Romans 5:20. Some time ago, a dear friend sent me an email with a profound insight into just how far God's grace extends:

"Why shouldn't we believe that Jesus' redemptive work is more powerful and effective than Satan's destructive work? Several years ago as I was working on a math book, I thought of an analogy that illustrates the verse 'Where sin did abound, grace did much more abound.' When I think about sin, it is so vast and overwhelming that its magnitude is on the scale of a googol – 10 to the 100th power, more than the number of elementary particles in the universe. A googol is a number that is so inconceivably huge that our minds cannot begin to grasp it.

"But the magnitude of grace is like a googolplex – 10 to the googol power, 1 with a googol of zeros after it, a number that dwarfs a googol into nothingness. As I imagine God's grace extending to every human being and defeating all the effects of sin and restoring every relationship – that is a heaven I can get excited about!"
- Diane Perkins Castro, personal correspondence

[272] God told Moses to tell the Israelites, *". . . I will free you from being slaves to them, and I will redeem you with an outstretched arm and*

with mighty acts of judgment. I will take you as my own people and I will be your God. Then you will know that I am the LORD your God, who brought you out from under the yoke of the Egyptians." – Exodus 6:6-8

[273] *". . . I will lay my hand on Egypt and with mighty acts of judgment I will bring out my divisions, my people the Israelites. And the Egyptians will know that I am the LORD when I stretch out my hand against Egypt and bring the Israelites out of it."* – Exodus 7:4-5

[274] Ezekiel 12:15-16

[275] Ezekiel 20:42-44

[276] Ezekiel 33:11

[277] Psalm 107:10-14. Verses 17-20 go on to say, *"Some became fools through their rebellious ways and suffered affliction because of their iniquities. They loathed all food and drew near the gates of death. Then they cried to the LORD in their trouble, and he saved them from their distress. He sent forth his word and healed them, he rescued them from the grave."*

[278] Psalm 107:43 – New Revised Standard Version

[279] Psalm 119:67, 71

[280] Proverbs 3:11-12

[281] *"The LORD . . . will cleanse the bloodstains from Jerusalem by a spirit of judgment and a spirit of fire."* – Isaiah 4:4

[282] *"I will refine and test them, for what else can I do because of the sin of My people? . . . I will make Jerusalem a heap of ruins, a haunt of jackals; and I will lay waste the towns of Judah so no one can live there."* – Jeremiah 9:7, 11

[283] *"I have surely heard Ephraim's moaning: 'You disciplined me like an unruly calf, and I have been disciplined. Restore me, and I will return, because you are the LORD my God. After I strayed, I repented; after I came to understand, I beat my breast. I was ashamed and humiliated because I bore the disgrace of my youth."* – Jeremiah 31:18-19

[284] Lamentations 3:31-33

[285] *"'Therefore wait for Me,' declares the LORD, 'for the day I will stand up to testify. I have decided to assemble the nations, to*

gather the kingdoms and to pour out my wrath on them – all my fierce anger. The whole world will be consumed by the fire of my jealous anger. Then will I purify the lips of the peoples, that all of them may call on the name of the LORD and serve Him shoulder to shoulder.'" – Zephaniah 3:8-9

[286] *"For he will be like a refiner's fire or a launderer's soap. He will sit as a refiner and purifier of silver; he will purify the Levites and refine them like gold and silver. Then the LORD will have men who will bring offerings in righteousness, and the offerings of Judah and Jerusalem will be acceptable to the LORD, as in days gone by, as in former years."* – Malachi 3:2-4

[287] I Corinthians 5:1

[288] I Corinthians 5:5 English Standard Version. He expresses a similar sentiment in I Timothy 1:20 about some who have rejected faith and a good conscience, and so have shipwrecked their faith – *"Among them are Hymenaeus and Alexander, who I have handed over to Satan to be taught not to blaspheme."*

[289] Hebrews 9:27

[290] I Timothy 2:3-6

[291] Psalm 62:11-12

[292] Genesis 1:1

[293] Daniel 5:21

[294] Proverbs 21:1

[295] Proverbs 21:30

[296] Psalm 135:6

[297] Ephesians 1:11

[298] Job 42:2

[299] Luke 1:37

[300] Jeremiah 32:27

[301] I John 4:16

[302] Psalm 145:8

[303] Psalm 145:9

[304] Deuteronomy 10:17

[305] Deuteronomy 10:18

[306] Luke 6:35

[307] Micah 7:18

[308] II Corinthians 1:3

[309] Lamentations 3:31-32

[310] Romans 2:11

[311] I Corinthians 13

[312] Isaiah 2:11-12 ESV

[313] Galatians 6:7 ESV

[314] Isaiah 13:11

[315] Isaiah 13:11

[316] I Peter 5:5

[317] Hebrews 12:29

[318] Hebrews 10:31 King James Version

[319] Luke 12:47-48

[320] I Timothy 1:15-16

Chapter 12 – But what about . . . ?

[321] Romans 4:20

[322] Romans 4:19

[323] Jesus' words are recorded in three different places in the Gospels – Matthew 12:31-32, Mark 3:28-29, and Luke 12:10.

[324] Mark 3:28-29. Matthew explains that anyone who speaks against the Holy Spirit will not be forgiven *"either in this age or in the age to come."* Luke simply says, *"anyone who blasphemes against the Holy Spirit will not be forgiven."*

[325] George MacDonald, *Unspoken Sermons*, Third Series, "Light," http://www.ccel.org/ccel/macdonald/unspoken3.ix.html,

[326] *"God raised us up with Christ and seated us with him in the heavenly realms in Christ Jesus in order that in the coming ages he might show the incomparable riches of his grace, expressed in his kindness to us in Christ Jesus."* – Ephesians 2:6-7

[327] Matthew 16:26

[328] *apollumi* in Greek

[329] W. E. Vine, *apollumi, An Expository Dictionary of New Testament Words*, Fleming H. Revell Company, Old Tappan, NJ, 1940, seventeenth impression 1966, p. 302

Cf. Oepke, *apollumi, The Theological Dictionary of The New Testament,* p. 396. The author comments, *"The word is not found in this sense* (ie eternal destruction) *in the apocr. and pseudepigr. Nor are there real equivalents in the Rabbis . . . It is striking that there are so few parallels in Str.-B. to the NT passages quoted."* The reason, of course, is because the word does not refer to eternal torment.

[330] Luke 5:37

[331] Luke 15:4, 6

[332] Luke 15:24

[333] Matthew 10:6.

Another clear example of the use of the word as it applies to people who "perish" is Luke 13:2-3, where Jesus answers some who had come to Him to tell Him about the Galileans whose blood Pilate had mixed with their sacrifices. Jesus responds by asking, *"Do you think that these Galileans were worse sinners than all the other Galileans because they suffered this way? I tell you, no! But unless you repent, you too will all perish."* It is clear from the context of this verse that Jesus is talking about perishing in a manner similar to the deaths of the unfortunate Galileans they had told Him about. Interestingly, Jesus' prediction was literally fulfilled when Jerusalem was destroyed by the Romans in AD 70. Many of the Jewish priests who were offering their sacrifices in the Temple were slain, and their blood mingled with the blood of the animals they were offering up.

[334] John 6:27

[335] Luke 13:23

[336] Luke 13:24-30

---

[337] Luke 13:23 – *The New Testament, An Expanded Translation*, Kenneth S. Wuest, William B. Eerdmans Publishing Company, Grand Rapids, MI, 1961, seventh printing, 1972, p. 173

[338] Matthew 7:13-14

[339] *"Rebekah's children had one and the same father, our father Isaac. Yet, before the twins were born or had done anything good or bad – in order that God's purpose in election might stand: not by works but by him who calls – she was told, 'The older will serve the younger.' Just as it is written: 'Jacob I loved, but Esau I hated.'"* – Romans 9:10-13

[340] Romans 9:22

[341] Malachi 1:2-3

[342] Cf. Bible Matters #9, by Gary Amirault, Tentmaker Ministries. http://www.tentmaker.org/Biblematters/hyperbole.htm

[343] Job 29:6

[344] Deuteronomy 1:28

[345] Luke 14:26

[346] Paul asks, *"What then shall we say? Is God unjust? Not at all! For he says to Moses, 'I will have mercy on whom I have mercy, and I will have compassion on whom I have compassion.' It does not, therefore, depend on man's desire or effort, but on God's mercy. For Scripture says to Pharaoh: "I raised you up for this very purpose, that I might display my power in you and that my name might be proclaimed in all the earth." Therefore God has mercy on whom he wants to have mercy, and he hardens whom he wants to harden."* – Romans 9:14-18

[347] Ephesians 2:3

[348] Paul makes it very clear that incorporating the Gentiles into His ultimate plan of salvation in no way means that God has completely and forever rejected the natural descendants of Abraham. *"Did God reject his people?"* Paul asks. *"By no means!"* is his answer. Paul himself is a natural descendant of Abraham, and God has always used a remnant of His people to accomplish His purposes. Regarding the Jews, he asks, *"Did they stumble so as to fall beyond recovery? Not at all! Rather, because of their transgression, salvation has come to the Gentiles . . ."* Just as God had borne with

patience the Gentiles who were objects of His wrath, so He will bear with patience the Jews.

[349] Romans 11:32

[350] Exodus 5:2

[351] Cf. Schmidt, *sklaruno,* Theological Dictionary of the New Testament, Vol. V, Wm. B. Eerdmans, 1967, p. 1030

[352] Exodus 10:1,7

[353] Exodus 7:5

[354] Romans 9:3. The word is also used in Acts 23:14 by the men who plotted to kill Paul, where it literally says, *"We have cursed ourselves with a curse."* The curse they placed upon themselves was to die physically from starvation and thirst if they did not kill Paul. It had nothing to do with being eternally condemned.

[355] Behm, *anathema, Theological Dictionary of the New Testament,* Volume 1, p. 354

[356] Ezekiel 33:11, 14-15

[357] Hebrews 6:4-6

[358] Cf. Hebrews 5:11-14

[359] Matthew 19:25-26

[360] Hebrews 6:4-6

[361] Or *fire and brimstone* in some versions

[362] Revelation 21:8
Regarding the Second Death referred to in this passage, Andrew Jukes, 19th century English clergyman, observed, *"The 'second death' therefore, so far from being, as some think, the hopeless shutting up of man forever in the curse of disobedience, will, if I err not, be God's way to free those who in no other way than by such a death can be delivered out of the dark world, whose life they live in. . . . And why should it be thought a thing incredible that God should raise the dead, who for their sin suffer the penalty of the second death? Does this death exceed the power of Christ to overcome it? Or shall the greater foe still triumph, while the less, the first death, is surely overcome? Who has taught us thus to limit the meaning of the words, 'Death is swallowed up in victory'?"* – Andrew Jukes, *The*

Second Death and the Restitution of All Things, Concordant Publishing Concern, Santa Clara, CA, republished 2001, pp. 91-92

[363] Revelation 20:10

[364] *Brimstone (theion)*, W.E. Vine, *An Expository Dictionary of New Testament Words*, Volume I, Fleming H. Revell Company, Old Tappan, NJ, p. 151

[365] http://www.georgiagulfsulfur.com/sulfur/history
The same uses were reported by Homer in the *Odyssey*.

[366] *basanos, basanizo,* Schneider, TDNT, Vol. I, Wm. B. Eerdmans Publishing Company, Grand Rapids, MI, 1964, eighth printing, August 1977, pp. 561-563.
It sometimes referred to torture in the ancient world, especially with slaves who testified in court, but the root sense is to prove the quality of as in the case of good versus forged money.

[367] Revelation 21:27

[368] Revelation 20:15

[369] John 3:3

[370] II Corinthians 5:17

[371] Luke 22:22 does not include the statement about it being better if Judas had not been born. It simply says, *"For the Son of Man goes as it has been determined, but woe to that man by whom he is betrayed!"*

[372] Matthew 26:24, English Standard Version

[373] When Job experienced the loss of his possessions, his children and his health, *"He said, May the day of my birth perish, and the night it was said, 'A boy is born!' That day – may it turn to darkness; may God above not care about it; may no light shine upon it. . . . May those who curse days curse that day . . . May its morning stars become dark; may it wait for daylight in vain and not see the first rays of dawn, for it did not shut the doors of the womb on me to hide trouble from my eyes."* – Job 3:2-10

Jeremiah, when overwhelmed by despair, complained to the Lord by cursing the day of his birth and the man who brought the news of his birth to Jeremiah's father. *"Cursed be the day I was born! May the day my mother bore me not be blessed! Cursed be the man who brought my father the news, who made him very glad, saying 'A child is born to you – a son!' . . . Why did I ever come out of the womb to see trouble and sorrow and to end my days in shame?"* – Jeremiah 20:15-18

Solomon used a similar expression when he observed, *"A man may have a hundred children and live many years; yet no matter how long he lives, if he cannot enjoy his prosperity and does not receive proper burial, I say that a stillborn child is better off than he."* – Ecclesiastes 6:3

[374] cf. Strong, *ouai*

[375] cf. Funk & Wagnalls Dictionary

[376] cf. Webster's Dictionary

[377] Matthew 27:3-5

[378] Cf. F.W. Farrar, *Mercy and Judgment*, MacMillan and Company, London, 1881, p. 459.
This understanding has translator support:
Wycliffe's translation of Matthew 26:24 reads, *". . . it were good to hym, if that man hadde not be borun."*
Young's Literal Translation reads, *"good it were for him if that man had not been born."*
The Douay-Reims Version translates the verse, *". . . it were better for him, if that man had not been born."*
The Revised Version New Testament of 1881 and the American Standard Version of 1901 put *"good for him if that man"* in the margin as an alternate rendering of the text.
Kenneth Wuest's *The New Testament: An Expanded Translation* reads, *"It would have been profitable for him if that man had not been born."*

[379] Luke 22:44

[380] II Corinthians 5:19-21

[381] *". . . you are heirs of the prophets and of the covenant God made with your fathers. He said to Abraham, 'Through your offspring all peoples on earth will be blessed.' When God raised up his servant, he sent him first to you to bless you by turning each of you from your wicked ways."* – Acts 3:25-26

[382] John 10:10

---

[383] St. Francis Xavier, *Letter from Japan, to the Society of Jesus in Europe, 1552*, The Internet Modern History Sourcebook, Fordham University,
http://www.fordham.edu/halsall/mod/1552xavier4.html

[384] Diane Perkins Castro, "The Unmentionable Subject," personal correspondence

Chapter 13 – How wide are heaven's doors . . . really?

[385] Luke 2:10-11.
That message was foreshadowed by God Himself when He told Abraham, *". . . all peoples on earth will be blessed through you."* – Genesis 12:3

[386] John 3:16

[387] John 3:17

[388] John 1:29

[389] John 12:32

[390] *"You gave him authority over everyone so that he could give eternal life to everyone you gave him."* – John 17:2, Common English Bible.

[391] *"This is good, and pleases God our Savior, who wants all people to be saved and to come to a knowledge of the truth. For there is one God and one mediator between God and mankind, the man Christ Jesus, who gave himself as a ransom for all people."* I Timothy 2:3-6 NIV 2011

[392] I Timothy 4:10 NIV 2011

[393] I John 2:2

[394] Adam and Eve were driven out of paradise . . . but they were *not* abandoned. God immediately implemented His plan to restore the human race – a plan that would center on a promised Child who would someday be born to the woman. – Genesis 3:15

[395] *"This is what the LORD says: 'Your wound is incurable, your injury beyond healing. There is no one to plead your cause, no remedy for your sore, no healing for you. All your allies have forgotten you; they care nothing for you. I have struck you as an*

enemy would and punished you as would the cruel, because your guilt is so great and your sins so many. . . . But I will restore you to health and heal your wounds,' declares the LORD . . . The fierce anger of the LORD will not turn back until he fully accomplishes the purposes of his heart. In days to come you will understand this." – Jeremiah 30:12-14, 17, 24

[396] Cf. II Chronicles 7:3

[397] This passage has often been misunderstood. God does *not* say that He punishes the children for the "sins" of the fathers, as if the innocent are punished for the sins of the guilty. Deuteronomy 24:16 makes it very clear that this is not to be done. *"Fathers shall not be put to death for their children, nor children put to death for their fathers; each is to die for his own sin."* Rather, God says that He will punish the children for the "sin" of the fathers. If a child continues in the same "sin" that his father engaged in, he, too, will be punished just as his father was. Those who sin will experience the consequences of their sin.

The focus of this revelation to Moses of the glory of the Lord is on God's mercy and love. He does not place a limit on His love – a love that extends to thousands of generations. It is on His punishment for sin that He places a limit.

[398] Psalm 103:8-14

[399] Micah 7:17-20

[400] Isaiah 25:6-8.

[401] Ezekiel 16:53-55

[402] I Corinthians 15:21-22
It's argued that the meaning of Paul's comment here is that in the same way that all who are *in Adam* die, so all who are *in Christ* will be made alive, thus limiting the extent of who will ultimately be saved to those who are *in Christ*. However, Paul did *not* say, *all who are in Christ will be made alive*. He said, *". . . in Christ all will be made alive."*

[403] Romans 5:20

[404] *"Does he not leave the ninety-nine in the open country and go after the lost sheep until he finds it?"* – Luke 15:4

[405] *"Does she not light a lamp, sweep the house and search carefully*

until she finds it?" – Luke 15:8

[406] Luke 15:20-24.
The father was *not* like the older brother who was willing for his sibling to remain forever away from his father's love . . . to suffer *endlessly* the painful consequences of his sinful choices.

[407] Luke 19:10

[408] John 12:31-32
The word Jesus used to describe what He would do – e*lkuso* – actually means *to drag.*

The same word is used in Acts 16:19 to describe the action of bringing Paul and Silas before the authorities. *"When the owners of the slave girl realized that their hope of making money was gone, they seized Paul and Silas and dragged (eilkusan) them into the marketplace to face the authorities."*

It is used again in Acts 21:30 when Paul was seen in the temple area in Jerusalem. His enemies stirred up the crowd against him and he was taken into custody. *"Seizing Paul, they dragged (eilkon) him from the temple, and immediately the gates were shut."*

In James 2:6 the same word is used to describe what the rich are doing to the poor: *"Is it not the rich who are exploiting you? Are they not the ones who are dragging (elkousin) you into court?"*

[409] Philippians 2:9-11

[410] Matthew 15:7-9

[411] *exomologeo* in Greek. This includes all uses of the related verb *homologeo* and the related noun *homologia.* In pointing this out, Thomas Johnson, Professor of Biblical Theology at George Fox University, commented, *"Inherent in the nature of confession is willing and, sometimes, joyful acknowledgement. It will not do to suppose that the humble confession of Phil. 2:11 is a reluctant and forced confession from Jesus' conquered enemies."* – Thomas Johnson, *Universal Salvation? The Current Debate*, William B. Eerdmans Publishing Company, Grand Rapids, MI/Cambridge, UK, 2003, p. 90

[412] Romans 5:6

[413] Romans 5:8

[414] Romans 5: 15, 18-20 NIV 2011

[415] *"For God has bound all men over to disobedience so that he may have mercy on them all." –* Romans 11:32
"Here, once again, we encounter a parallel structure where the first 'all' determines the reference of the second. According to Paul, the very ones whom God 'shuts up' to disobedience – whom he blinds, or hardens, or cuts off for a season – are those to whom he is merciful . . . God hardens a heart in order to produce, in the end, a contrite spirit, blinds those who are unready for the truth in order to bring them ultimately to the truth, 'imprisons all in disobedience so that he may be merciful to all.'" – Thomas Talbott, *Universal Salvation: The Current Debate*, Edited by Robin A. Parry and Christopher Hugh Partridge, Wm. B. Eerdmans Publishing Company, 2004, p. 34

[416] Romans 12:21

[417] II Corinthians 5:19

[418] Colossians 1:16-18, 20
[419] Acts 3:21

[420] Ephesians 1:9-10

[421] Gerry Beauchemin, *Hope Beyond Hell*, Malista Press, Olmito, TX, p. 111

[422] Revelation 5:13

[423] We're told that the city *". . . shone with the glory of God, and its brilliance was like that of a very precious jewel. . . It had a great, high wall with twelve gates, and with twelve angels at the gates . . . The foundations of the city walls were decorated with every kind of precious stone . . . The city does not need the sun or the moon to shine on it, for the glory of God gives it light . . . Nothing impure will ever enter it, nor will anyone who does what is shameful or deceitful, but only those whose names are written in the Lamb's book of life . . . Then the angel showed me the river of the water of life, as clear as crystal, flowing from the throne of God and of the Lamb down the middle of the great street of the city. On each side of the river stood the tree of life, bearing twelve crops of fruit, yielding its fruit every month. And the leaves of the tree are for the healing of the nations. No longer will there be any curse."* – Revelation 21:11-12, 19, 23, 27; 22:1-3

[424] Revelation 22:14

[425] *"Outside are the dogs, those who practice magic arts, the sexually immoral, the murderers, the idolaters and everyone who loves and practices falsehood."* – Revelation 22:15

[426] Revelation 22:17

[427] Revelation 22:17; for a universalist interpretation of the book of Revelation, see Gregory MacDonald (pseudonym for Robin Parry), *The Evangelical Universalist*, Cascade Books, Eugene, OR, 2006

A final word

[428] I Corinthians 15:28

[429] Genesis 1:31

Acknowledgments

I began writing this book in earnest 10 years ago, but it started out almost 40 years ago as a research paper for a class in seminary.

God graciously provided a professor who was an honest scholar, and who later became a dear friend. He doesn't agree with my conclusions and asked that I not include his name in the book. Still, if he hadn't been someone I could trust at the time, this book would never have been written. I'm also grateful for my parents-in-law, Gerald and Violet Vaculik. They encouraged me to go to seminary and provided the means to make it happen.

The first person I ever talked to who believed in the ultimate restoration of all was Gary Amirault – 29 years after I wrote my paper. His website, *Tentmaker.org*, is a treasure trove of information on the subject. Gary suggested I read Gerry Beauchemin's book, *Hope Beyond Hell!* I had previously believed that there was room within Scripture to believe in ultimate restoration. Gerry's book convinced me that it was what Scripture actually taught. Gary and Gerry, I am grateful for you both.

Jennifer Schuckmann, Jill Lamar and Diane Perkins Castro were a tremendous source of encouragement when I first began writing. Jennifer provided a wealth of knowledge about the publishing industry and introduced me to several very important people. Jill felt what I wrote needed to be said. Diane copyedited the first draft of my book, consistently encouraged me to keep going when things didn't go the way I had hoped, and shared a number of insights that have made the book better.

Along the way, I met great people in the publishing industry whose encouragement, insights and help were invaluable. Thank you Carolyn McCready, Ken Peterson, Wes Yoder and David McCormick.

Several noted scholars were kind enough to offer encouragement and helpful suggestions. Some agreed with my conclusions, some did not. Thank you I. Howard Marshall, Fr. Brian E. Daley, Gabriel Fackre, Perry G. Phillips, Nigel G. Wright, John Sanders, Randy Sachs, Robin Parry, Randal Rauser, and Ilaria Ramelli. Time is our most valuable possession, I'm grateful to each of you for giving me some of your valuable time. David Konstan was gracious enough to not only read my manuscript and share his encouraging comments, he also allowed me to put his words on the cover. Thank you, David.

Carol McCauley has been a tremendous blessing. Carol was the one who initially contacted me about reconnecting with her brother Jack, a former roommate in college. When she first learned of my book, she was certain that my position on restoration was wrong . . . until she read the book. Then, she and her husband, Ray, became two of my most ardent supporters. I'm also grateful for Terry Kersey's insights, ideas and observations.

It's been said that you shouldn't judge a book by its cover. That may be true, but a good cover is eye-catching, and a great cover hints at the content of the book to entice readers graphically. The combination of striking colors and a simple star on the cover of *Heaven's Doors* does both. Plus, the continuity of the star throughout the text begins every chapter with a reminder of hope. I'm grateful to Fred Daunno for the time, effort and creativity he gave my book because he believed in it.

Acknowledgments

Computers have become indispensable tools for researching, writing and publishing a book. My son, Will, and my daughter, Jane, have been my technical advisers. Will installed and taught me how to use various computer programs, and Jane was always there when I needed to ask, "How do I do this?" My cousin, Georgia Brownstein, provided indispensable information about publishing and social marketing.

Steven Arcieri is my friend and the best voiceover talent agent in New York. Lately, he stepped in to be an effective literary agent, as well. He's always been supportive. He's always been helpful in any way necessary. And he's always given me wise advice. He's one of the greatest blessings in my life.

During the course of researching and writing this book, I lost friends, a job, and a church family. I also gained much that made it well worthwhile. But, I was not alone on my journey. The things that happened to me also directly affected my wife, Suzan. Her consistent support and encouragement throughout our 45 years of marriage has shown me how truly valuable a wife of noble character really is.

"Thank you, Lord, for Suzan."

While eating breakfast on July 19, 2012, my former college roommate who I hadn't spoken to in 42 years called to wish me a happy birthday. We reconnected as a result. And Jack Linn has been the best editor, copyeditor, marketing guru and friend I could ever have asked for. More than anyone else, he's been instrumental in making the message of this book clear and understandable for everyone who picks it up. His fingerprints are literally on every single page.

"Thank you, God, for Jack."

Praise for George W. Sarris'
Unique Storytelling

"I grew up thinking the Bible is dull. Thank you for helping us teach our children otherwise."
Helen
Spokane, WA

"Your Bible stories tape received the ultimate compliment yesterday. A car full of 8 to 10-year-old boys sat absolutely quiet for 30 minutes, spellbound by your dramatic portrayal of the stories from Daniel."
Judy
Perry, GA

"I am thrilled that the kids are memorizing Scripture as they listen over & over. Your interpretation and portrayal of characters is wonderful and makes it exciting to listen to, not just for the kids, but for parents too."
Brenda
Clark Summit, PA

"You truly have influenced our children's lives with the Scripture you have brought to life for them. Thank you!"
Laura
Lauren, MS

"George W. Sarris' one-person dramatizations of the Bible are so real that it makes you feel as though you are there. I highly recommend them."
William R. Bright
Founder, Campus Crusade for Christ

Hear a Sample and Order Today!
WorldsGreatestStories.com

Made in the USA
Middletown, DE
17 July 2022